I0474000

INNOVATION & KNOWLEDGE

ECONOMICS

Argentino Pessoa
University of Porto

Copyright © 2012 Argentino Pessoa
All rights reserved.
ISBN-10: 147508806X
ISBN-13: 978-1475088069
Cover design: Ana Pessoa
Printed in the US by CreateSpace, Charleston, SC.

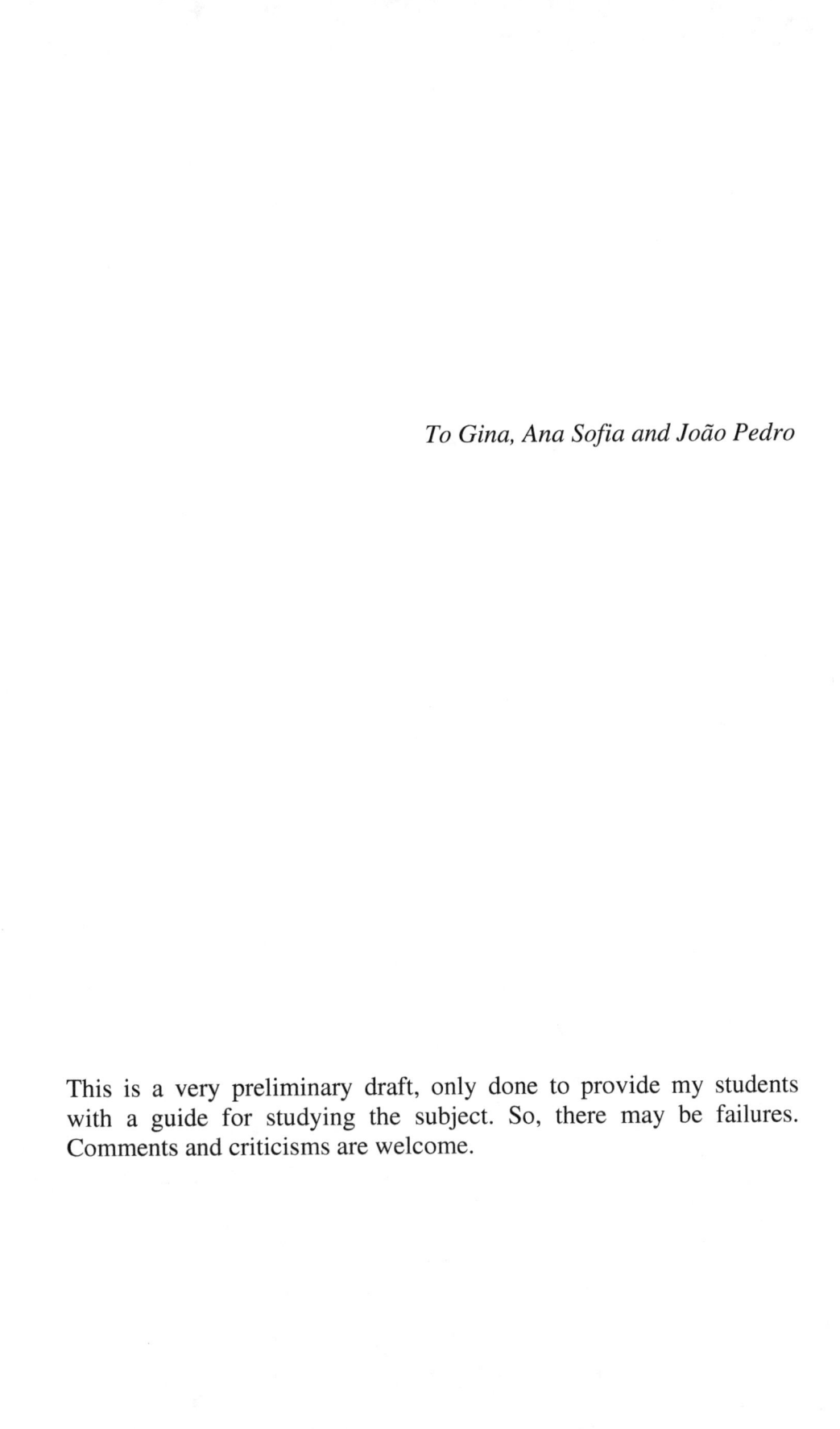

To Gina, Ana Sofia and João Pedro

This is a very preliminary draft, only done to provide my students with a guide for studying the subject. So, there may be failures. Comments and criticisms are welcome.

CONTENTS

Index of boxes, tables and figures

Figures

ACRONYMS AND ABBREVIATIONS

BERD	Expenditure on R&D in the Business Enterprise Sector
EPO	European Patent Office
FDI	Foreign Direct Investment
FTE	Full-time Equivalent (on R&D)
GBAORD	Government Budget Appropriations or Outlays for R&D
GDP	Gross Domestic Product
GERD	Gross Domestic Expenditure on R&D
GOVERD	Government Intramural Expenditure on R&D
GUF	General University Funds
HERD	Expenditure on R&D in the Higher Education Sector
ID	Industrial District
IPRs	Intellectual property rights
IS	Innovation System
ISIC	International Standard Industrial Classification
NIS	National Innovation System
NSE	Natural Sciences and Engineering
OECD	Organization for Economic Co-operation and Development
PCT	Patent Co-operation Treaty
PNP	Private Non-Profit Institutions
PPP	Purchasing Power Parities
R&D	Research and Experimental Development
RIS	Regional Innovation System
SITC	Standard International Trade Classification
SME	Small and Medium Enterprise
SSH	Social Sciences and Humanities
STI	Science, Technology and Innovation
TBP	Technology Balance of Payments
TFP	Total Factor Productivity
USPTO	United States Patent and Trademark Office
WIPO	World Intellectual Property Organisation

PREFACE

This book examines the chief perspectives that have emerged along time, and particularly in the last decades, about the role of innovation in the economy and in society. My aim in writing it is to provide readers with the needed instruments to answer questions such us: what is innovation? How does innovation contribute to the different economies' performance? What is the source of innovative capability occurring in different sectors, regions and countries? How does research and science affect innovation? What is the policy role in supporting innovation?

In order to answer the above questions in a systematic way, the book is organized in seven chapters. Chapter one deals with definitions and measurement problems associated to the innovation process. Hence, after distinguishing between invention, and innovation and diffusion, two topics are presented: the Freeman taxonomy of technical change and the modeling of the innovation process. In relation to the latter topic, both the linear model and the interactive model of innovation are presented, underlining the contrast between them. The remainder of the chapter is totally dedicated to the STI (Science, Technology and Innovation) measurement. The most recognized indicators are presented, both in terms of input and in terms of output of STI, and their usefulness and limitations in international comparisons are underlined.

The chapter two relates innovation with economic dynamics. It begins by presenting the similarities of innovation, economic growth and structural change. Then the chapter proceeds to analyze the seminal approach of Schumpeter concerning innovation, economic development and business cycles. Next, the concept of techno-economic paradigm is introduced and some explanations about the relationship between innovation and long cycles are provided for. The chapter ends by presenting the technology gap model of Jan Fagerberg.

Chapter three is dedicated to the economic foundations of innovation and diffusion. Beginning with the evolutionary approach to the innovation process, emphasis is placed on the dissimilarity between this approach and the mainstream theory. Next, two other controversies are introduced: the technology-push vs. demand-pull debate and the induced technological change argument. The remainder of the chapter deals with the technology diffusion and with the explanations for the pattern that technology adoption usually presents: the S curve.

Chapter four deals with the sectoral patterns of innovation. Appropriability, technological opportunity and cumulativeness are some concepts introduced and the usefulness of these is demonstrated with the definition of innovation patterns and technological regimes. Next, the Pavitt's taxonomy based on the techno-economic characteristics of industries is presented, not only in the static version but also dynamically, as a contribution to a successful technology policy of development in late industrialized countries.

Chapter five explains the territorial foundations of innovation. Beginning with the association of the territory to the production of external economies for firms and industries, the chapter proceeds with a reflection about the relevance of some concepts associated to the territorial location of economic activities. Proximity, tacit knowledge, network, innovative milieu and industrial district are some such concepts which are presented and explained as sources of both static and dynamic efficiency. A reflection about the relationship between knowledge base and competitiveness and the Richard Florida's view about creative cities conclude the chapter.

Innovation systems are the focus of the chapter six. Beginning with the concept and functions of the innovation system and by distinguishing several systems of innovation with a particular emphasis on the difference between national and regional system, the creative cities and knowledge base perspectives are retaken and discussed in the light of the regional innovation system concept. The

Asheim and Gertler's taxonomy of regional systems of innovation closes the chapter.

Finally, the book ends with a chapter focused on a preliminary approach to the innovation policy. Together with the presentation of several policy instruments, the foundations of innovation policy, the appropriability problem, the intellectual property problematic, the difference between private and social return of innovative activities, as well as the trade-off between static and dynamic efficiency are some of the various issues taken in hand.

Chapter 1
CONCEPTS AND MEASUREMENT

Summary
Concepts: Invention, innovation and diffusion. Technological innovation and other types of innovation. Innovation taxonomy. Models of innovation.
Science, technology and innovation: concepts and problems of measurement. Input and output indicators.
The Innovation Union Scoreboard.

1.1. Concepts

The word innovation is usually used with two different but related meanings. It can designate either a process — the process of innovation— or a phase of the process. Looking at the innovation process as if it was a "black box" has a long tradition in the economics profession. In fact, the traditional view considers innovation and technological activity as a black box, wherein it is something that is only of the interest of Scientists and Engineers; economists must only deal with what enters and goes out the box, that is with inputs and outputs of technological activity. This is a very static approach, which is well accommodated by the neoclassical theory of equilibrium. However, Joseph Schumpeter was the first author that criticized the static nature of the mainstream economics by looking at inside the black box. This Austrian economist published at the beginning of the 20th. Century a fundamental book titled *The Theory of Economic Development* (Schumpeter, 1911), where the economic development is linked to the innovation process for the first time.

According to Schumpeter, the beginning of a development process occurs precisely in the sphere of production as a consequence of innovations. These are facts that decisively and deeply alter the old productive systems.

Schumpeter was also the first author to establish a difference between the three phases of the innovation process: Invention, innovation and diffusion. In his view an invention corresponds to something new. It implies an advance in scientific or technical knowledge, and so, it can contribute to technological change. But this does not mean that the invention must have an economic utilization. Often, but not always, the invention is the result of research and experimental development and is produced by scientists and engineers. Many inventions are not used in the economy and, as a result, they affect neither the economic system nor the productivity of the economy. So, inventions only have economic impact if they are used in new goods, new productive processes or new forms of organization and management.

By definition, innovation is the first economic application of a given invention. It is the introduction of new knowledge in the economy. Usually, it is accepted that this new knowledge is embodied in goods and productive processes, originating technological innovations (innovation-product and innovation process, respectively). But innovation is not limited to the technological domain, it can also be related with organization and management, as the Schumpeterian typology shows.

1.1.1. Types of innovation

In fact, in his *Theory of Economic Development*, Schumpeter classifies innovations in 5 types, as in the following way:

* Introduction of a *new good* in the economy, that is a good that is not known by consumers, or the introduction of a new quality in a pre-existent good;
* Introduction of a *new process* of production, *i.e.*, a technique of production not yet verified by experience. This must not need to result from any scientific discovery, but can merely consist in a new method of commercialization of a given good;
* The opening of a *new market*, that is a "new" market for a specific industry in the sense that the products of this industry have never had access to it before, independently of whether this market has previously existed or not;
* The conquest of a *new source of supply,* either of raw materials or half-manufactured goods, independently of this source having previously existed or being now created;
* The carrying out of the *new organization* of any industry as, for instance, the creation or the rupture of a monopolistic position.

1.1.2. Innovation, entrepreneur, profit and development

For the new combinations to be carried into effect, Schumpeter first emphasized the role of the entrepreneur as the central change-maker. Schumpeter calls "entrepreneur act" to the introduction of an innovation in the economic system and "entrepreneur" to the person that carries out this act. According to Schumpeter, enterprise and entrepreneur are specific facts of development and are non-existent in the stationary state, where the direction of production only implies a routine activity indistinguishable from any other type of work.

The aim of the entrepreneurial activity is profit. The most obvious example of a profitable innovation is the production of a commonly used good for a reduced unitary cost than the one paid to the other firms. This happens because the innovator uses a new method that allows one unit of product to be obtained from a lower quantity of a given factor, or from a lower amount of all the production factors. In this case the entrepreneur will buy the needed inputs at the same prices of the other firms and will sell his goods to the current price, which is the same price that the other established firms use. So his gains are higher than his costs and it is this difference that is profit. Other two types of innovation (new organization of production and the discovery of a new source, cheaper, of the supply of productive resources) are profitable in the same way as the above-mentioned innovation.

When innovation consists of introducing a new good which presents an increased satisfaction of consumer needs relatively to the one of current production, the possibility of profit arises from the fact that the higher level of satisfaction allows the entrepreneur to ask for a higher price, which surpasses costs relatively to the price of old goods. In the case of the discovery of new markets, or when new goods are created to satisfy needs not previously satisfied, initially prices have no connection with costs, and potential buyers are willing to pay a price higher than the cost.

In the stationary state, as there are no innovations, there is no profit. Although profit is a typical phenomenon of development, which is condemned to disappear with the development, the development reconstructs continuously the conditions to its reappearance. When an innovation is successful, other firms try to imitate the pioneer innovator. This imitation initiates a process of diffusion, where other firms adopt the innovation and, consequently, it is spread to the rest of the economy (across firms, sectors, regions and even across countries).

In fact, since profit appears at a point of the system, the condition that originates it (the innovation) begins its diffusion, and when the diffusion is generalized, the competitive process that relates prices with costs will imply the disappearance of profit. However, this vanishing is only apparent from the point of view of the firm because actually the profit, far from disappearing, extends to the whole economic system, by increasing wealth in the same amount as the production effort.

From the viewpoint of the firm, if the innovation stream does not stop, profit always reappears. Naturally, it is always possible, and it often happens, that the competitive mechanism does not work perfectly. In this case, the profit, or a part of it, is not diffused all over the economic system and tends to remain within the firm. In this case it loses the nature of profit, as it is not the result of innovative acts and only exists because of routine actions, being therefore more exactly classified as a monopoly rent.

The above explanation provides a reason for deciding to innovate. Firms innovate to defend their competitive position as well as to seek competitive advantage. A firm may take a reactive approach by innovating to prevent losing market share to an innovative competitor. Or it may take a proactive approach to gain a strategic market position relative to its competitors, for example by developing and then trying to enforce higher technical standards for the goods it produces. So, technical change is far from straightforward. New technologies compete with established ones, and in many cases replace them. These processes of *technological diffusion* are often long lasting, and usually involve incremental improvement both to new and established technologies.

1.1.3. The Freeman's taxonomy

Different innovations have different impact on productivity and well-being. After Schumpeter, other economists identified several kinds of innovations (Mensch, 1979; Dosi, 1988; Clark, 1985;

Freeman, 1984). Freeman *et al.* (1982), Freeman and Soete (1987) and Freeman and Perez categorize various types of technical change in the typology known as the Freeman's taxonomy. In this taxonomy innovations and technical change are classified as:

1. **Incremental innovations**. These occur more or less continuously in any industry or service activity, although at a varying rate in different industries and over different time periods. They may often occur, not so much as the result of formal research and development activity, but as the outcome of inventions and improvements suggested by engineers and others directly engaged in the production process, or as a result of initiatives and proposals by users. Many empirical studies have confirmed their great importance in improving the efficiency in the use of all factors of production. Incremental innovations are frequently associated with the scaling up of plant and equipment, as well as to quality improvements of products and services. They are particularly important in the period after the success of a radical innovation. Although their combined effect is extremely important in the growth of productivity, no single incremental innovation has dramatic effects, and they may sometimes pass unnoticed and unrecorded. However, their effects are apparent in the steady growth of productivity, which is reflected in input-output tables over time by major changes in the coefficients for the existing array of products and services (Freeman et al., 1982).

2. **Radical innovations**. These are discontinuous events. in recent times they are usually the result of deliberate research and development activity in enterprises and/or in universities and government laboratories. They are unevenly distributed over sectors and over time. Some authors (e.g., Mensch, 1979) consider that their appearance is concentrated particularly in periods of deep recessions. However what appears as consensual is the idea that, whenever they may occur, they are important as the potential catalyst for the growth of new markets, or for big improvements in the cost and quality of existing products. Over a period of decades a radical innovation, such as nylon or the contraceptive pill, may

have fairly dramatic effects, but in terms of their economic impact they are relatively small and localized, unless a whole cluster of radical innovations are linked together in the rise of entire new industries and services, such as the synthetic materials industry or the semiconductor industry. Strictly speaking, at a sufficiently disaggregate level, radical innovations would constantly require the addition of new rows and columns in an input-output table. But in practical terms, such changes are introduced only in the case of the most important innovations and with long time-lags, when their economic impact is already substantial (Freeman et al., 1982).

3. **New technological systems** are 'constellations' of innovations (Keirstead, 1948) technically and economically inter-related. Obvious examples are the clusters of synthetic materials innovations and petrochemical innovations in the 1930s, 1940s and 1950s. They include numerous radical and incremental innovations in both products and processes (Freeman *et al.*, 1982).

4. **Changes of techno-economic paradigm**. These are also known as technological revolutions since they are far-reaching and pervasive changes in technology which affect many (or even all) branches of the economy and generate entirely new sectors. Examples given by Schumpeter are the steam engine and electric power. Characteristic of this type of technical change is that it affects the input cost structure and the conditions of production and distribution for almost every branch of the economy (Freeman *et al.*, 1982). A change in techno-economic paradigm thus comprises clusters of radical and incremental innovations and embraces several 'new technology systems'.

There are other concepts which present similarities with the ones of the Freeman's taxonomy. For instance, Bresnahan and Trajtenberg (1995) state that technical progress and growth appear to be driven by a few "General Purpose Technologies" (GPTs) such as the stream engine, the electric motor and semiconductors. GPTs are surely involved in changes of techno-economic paradigm as they are characterized by pervasiveness, inherent potential for technical improvements, and complementarities, giving rise to increasing returns-to-scale.

Dosi (1982) uses the expression 'change of technological paradigm' and makes comparisons with the analogous approach of Kuhn (1962) to 'scientific revolutions' and paradigm changes in basic science. In these terms 'incremental innovation' along established technological trajectories may be compared with Kuhn's normal science. At the same time as there are similarities in all these concepts, the approach of Perez (1985) is the most systematic and has some important distinguishing features. She argues that the development of a new "techno-economic paradigm" involves a new "best practice" set of rules and customs for designers, engineers, entrepreneurs and managers which differs from the previously prevailing paradigm.

To sum up, changes of techno-economic paradigm are based on combinations of radical product, process and organizational innovations. They occur relatively seldom (perhaps twice in a century) but when they occur they necessitate changes in the institutional and social framework, as well as in most enterprises if their potential is to be fully exploited. They give rise to major changes in the organizational structure of firms, the skill mix and the management style of industry.

It is noteworthy that nothing is said so far about what is being changed, or in what sense the change is taking place. Nelson and Winter (1982) introduced the concept of technological trajectories to describe both continuous changes and discontinuities in technological innovations: continuous changes are often related to progress along a technological trajectory – the direction of advance within a technological paradigm – while discontinuities are associated with the emergence of a new technological paradigm.

As we will see later, technological innovation may originate from two forces: market pull versus technology push. It is possible to make an association between these forces and the two first types in the Freeman Taxonomy: incremental and radical innovation. Dosi (1988) states that an incremental innovation is more likely to be a market pull innovation, while a radical innovation is generally originated by scientists and often incorporates new technologies or new combinations of existing technologies. As a consequence, radical innovation is often a technology push innovation.

1.1.4. Models of innovation

We must distinguish the need to identify the different phases of the innovation process, which is justified in academic terms, from the so-called 'linear model' of innovation, which postulates a deterministic sequential order between phases. The "linear model" basically means a linear impact of science and technology on economic development (Figure 1.1).

Figure 1.1.
Linear model of innovation

| Research | → | Development | → | Design | → | Production | → | Marketing |

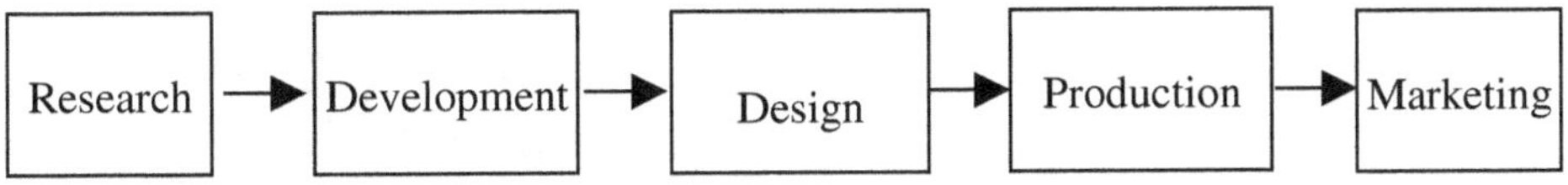

The main assumption underlying this model is that research carried out by researchers/scientists leads to a new idea, which becomes a new product, for which a production process is developed by industrial engineers, and for which a marketing plan is then set up, conducting to its increasing demand in the market.

Figure 1.2:
An interactive model of the innovation process

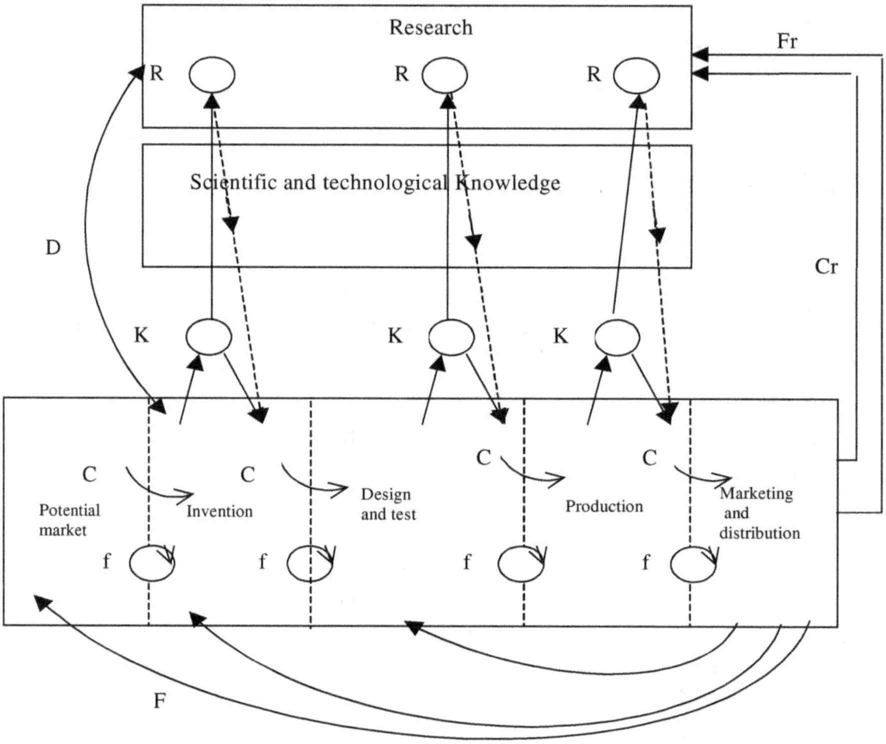

Symbols used:
Horizontal links
•   C = central chain of innovation
•   f = Feedback loops.
•   F = Particularly important feedback.
Vertical links:
•   K-R = Links through knowledge to research and return paths.
•   D = Direct link to and from research from problems in invention and design.
•   Cr = Contribution of the manufacturing sector scientific research by instruments, procedures of technology, etc.
•   Fr = Financial support of research by firms in sciences underlying product area.

Source: adapted from Kline and Rosenberg (1986).

A policy implication of the linear model is that to propel innovation and productivity, supporting research through financial incentives is enough. Nowadays, a large consensus exists that the linear model of innovation cannot be an accurate picture of the innovation process. So, authors usually use a more complex model to represent the innovation process. A model with a central chain of innovation, linked to the research activity and several nodes and not always active links.

Figure 1.2 represents an adaptation of the model presented by Kline e Rosenberg (1986) — the chain-linked model—, which is one of the most well-known in the economics of innovation. As is apparent from the figure, there are several direct and indirect links and feedbacks.

1.2. Science, technology and innovation

The first collection of statistics on science, technology and innovation (STI) has more than a century. From then on some improvements were introduced in the data collected, but statistics on this topic go on being much deficient. In fact, James Cattell the editor of *Science* for fifty years (1895-1944), has published in 1906 the first compilation of scientists, entitled *American Men of Science*, and, based on that list, Cattell has regularly published statistical analyses for thirty years on what he called the performance of scientists. Also in the early 1900s, some psychologists began counting scientific papers (thus appearing bibliometrics), as a tool for measuring the advancement of psychology as a science.

From these very first exercises, the measurement of science, technology and innovation has changed considerably. At its very beginning, statistics was concerned with measuring the size of the scientific community (counting the number of "men of science") and scientists' activities (counting papers). Scientists themselves, among them psychologists and geographers, conducted the measurements. In the early 1920s, these statistics and their sources became institutionalized and, from the 1940s to the 1950s, new ones were constructed. However, scientists no longer produced these new statistics, instead government departments and national bureaus of statistics proceeded to collection.

The main works conducted by these public institutions, unlike previous measurements, dealt with measuring a "national budget for science" by counting the money devoted to R&D. The focus was no longer exclusively on universities, as Cattell's had been, but on all economic sectors: industry, government, university, and non-profit organizations. The focus was no longer on "men of science" but on organizations and their R&D activities. Above all, the focus was on measuring the efficiency or "productivity" of the S&T (science and technology) system, defined as the output arising from research activities.

1.2.1. Measuring the S&T activity

The first formal efforts for measuring the S&T activity were made by a small number of countries, including the United States, the United Kingdom, the Netherlands, Japan, Canada and France which were encouraged by the rapid growth of the amount of national resources devoted to research and experimental development (R&D). Following these pioneering efforts, other OECD member countries began to collect statistical data in this field around 1960. However, they encountered theoretical difficulties when starting R&D surveys, as differences in scope, methods and concepts made international comparisons difficult. The need for some attempt at standardization of the kind undertaken for economic statistics was increasingly felt and, in June 1963, the OECD met with national experts on R&D (research and development) statistics at the Villa Falcioneri in Frascati, Italy.

The result was the first official version of the *Proposed Standard Practice for Surveys of Research and Development*, usually known as the *Frascati Manual*.

Today's R&D statistics are the result of the systematic development of surveys based on the *Frascati Manual* and are now part of the statistical system of the OECD member countries. Although the Manual is basically a technical document, it is also a basis for OECD efforts to increase the understanding of the role played by science and technology by analyzing national systems of innovation. Given the importance of the manual, the basis for collecting data on research and innovation is known as the "Frascati Family". This includes not only the Frascati Manual (on R&D) but also the Canberra Manual (about human resources), the Oslo Manual (on innovation), and other manuals respecting technological balance of payments and patents.

By providing internationally accepted definitions of R&D and classifications of its component activities, the *Frascati Manual* contributes to intergovernmental discussions on "best practices" for science and technology policies. But the Frascati Manual is a standard for R&D surveys, not only in OECD member countries. As a result of initiatives by the UNESCO, the European Union and various regional organizations, the *Frascati Family* has become a standard for R&D surveys worldwide.

In the past, most of the work on S&T indicators has been based on an Input/output model, where the indicators are structured along the categories of 'input' and 'ouput' (figure 1.3), following a production function logic, in a national accounts paradigm, that is the level of analysis is the country and the indicators are built as aggregates at this level, the individual agents disappear and the national innovation system is reduced to a single point, described in its different aspects. This approach also corresponds to the idea that innovation process is a "black box", with an interior beyond the economist understanding.

13

In the center of the figure is a box with the three phases of the innovation process as we have seen in section (1.1) — invention, innovation and diffusion — preceded by an R&D stage, in a linear model tradition. Both the R&D expenditures and the R&D personnel are contributing to the increase in the activity that takes place inside the box, and so the economist must measure such inputs.

Figure 1.3.
The measurement of Science, Technology and Innovation

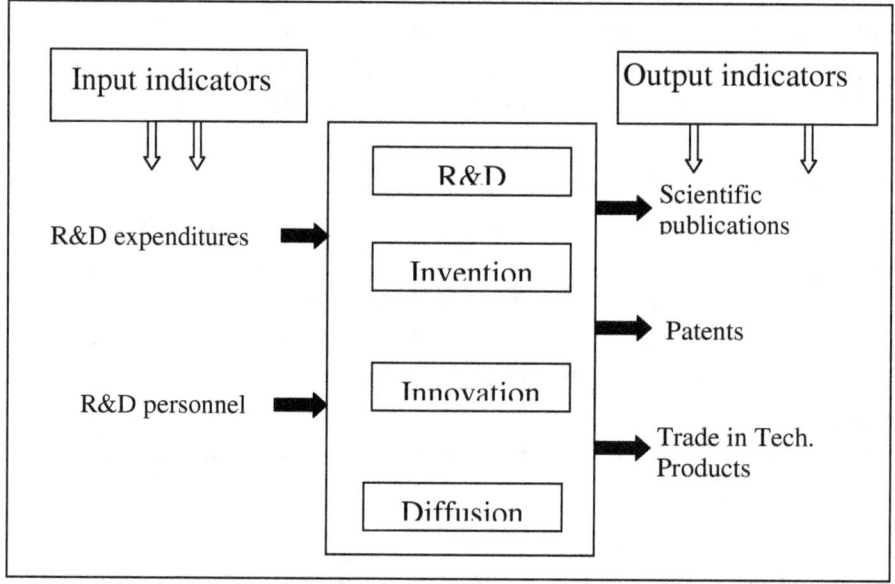

With the same rationale, the output of R&D, or science and technology (S&T) in general, can be measured in several ways: the economist must look at the outputs of the box, with patents, scientific publications and trade in technological products as the most commonly recognized outcomes of the process. More recently, efforts are made for measuring innovation itself. Thus innovation surveys are an attempt to measure outputs and the effects of the innovation process in which R&D plays an important role. A manual on innovation surveys has been issued and revised once (OECD, 1997a).

The statistics on S&T have reached a mature stage, with a clear division of work between international agencies like OECD and Eurostat playing a role of harmonization and of production of international comparative statistics, while national statistical agencies are in charge of collecting and elaborating data at national level. However, some shortcomings in the quality and comparability of data remain. One such shortcomings is the periodicity (or its absence) in data collection. R&D data collection has not the same time regularity as other national accounts statistics (e.g., GDP data) do.

1.2.2. Input indicators

1.2.2.1. R&D expenditures

The main expenditure aggregate used for international comparisons is the gross domestic expenditure on R&D (GERD), which covers all expenditures for R&D performed on national territory in a given year. It thus includes domestically performed R&D which is financed from abroad but excludes R&D funds paid abroad, notably to international agencies. The corresponding personnel measure does not have a special name. It covers total personnel working on R&D on national territory during a given year. International comparisons are sometimes restricted to researchers (or university graduates) because it is considered that they are the true core of the R&D system. In what follows we give a snapshot of each one of the most used R&D indicators, beginning by the most known, GERD.

According to the *Frascati* manual, Research and experimental development (R&D) comprise creative work undertaken on a systematic basis in order to increase the stock of knowledge, including knowledge of man, culture and society, and the use of this stock of knowledge to devise new applications[1]. For statistical purposes, two types of inputs are measured: R&D expenditures and R&D personnel. Both inputs are normally measured on an annual basis: so much spent during a year, so many person-years used during a year. Both series have their strengths and weaknesses, and, in consequence, both are necessary to secure an adequate representation of the effort devoted to R&D. The basic measure is "intramural expenditures"; *i.e.* all expenditures for R&D performed within a statistical unit or sector of the economy[2]. For R&D purposes, both current costs and capital expenditures are measured. In the case of the government sector, expenditures refer to direct rather than indirect expenditures. Depreciation costs are excluded.

Guidelines are suggested for the treatment of public general university funds (GUF), also called general university funds, *i.e.,* that part of university research which is financed from the general grant from ministries of education, which is destined for both education and research. Such flows may represent up to over half of all support for university research and are an important share of all public support for R&D. R&D covers both formal R&D in R&D units and informal or occasional R&D in other units. However, interest in R&D depends more on the new knowledge and innovations and the economic and social effects that result rather than on the activity itself.

R&D must be distinguished from a wide range of related activities with a scientific and technological basis. These other activities are very closely linked to R&D, both through flows of

---

[1] The first two versions of the Frascati manual covered only the natural sciences and engineering. The social sciences and humanities were incorporated in the third edition (OECD, 1976), adopted in 1974.

[2] A statistical unit may have expenditures on R&D either within the unit (intramural) or outside it (extramural). The full procedure for measuring these expenditures is as follows: Intramural expenditures are all expenditures for R&D performed within a statistical unit or sector of the economy during a specific period, whatever the source of funds. Extramural expenditures are the sums a unit, organisation or sector reports having paid or committed themselves to pay to another unit, organisation or sector for the performance of R&D during a specific period.

information and in terms of operations, institutions and personnel, but as far as possible, the following activities should be excluded when measuring R&D.

All education and training of personnel in the natural sciences, engineering, medicine, agriculture, the social sciences and the humanities in universities and special institutions of higher and post-secondary education should be excluded from GERD. The only exception is the research made by students at the PhD level carried out at universities. Also the service of Scientific and technical information, as well as the specialized activities of Collecting, Coding, Recording, Classifying, Disseminating, Translating, Analyzing and Evaluating by Scientific and technical personnel are to be excluded, except when conducted solely or primarily for the purpose of R&D support (*e.g.* the preparation of the original report of R&D findings should be included in R&D). Also general-purpose data collection undertaken by government agencies to record natural, biological or social phenomena that is of general public interest (routine topographical mapping; routine geological, hydrological, oceanographic and meteorological surveying, etc). The guiding principle is always the same: only data collected solely or primarily as part of the R&D process are included in GERD. The same reasoning applies to the processing and interpretation of the data. The social sciences, in particular, are very dependent on an accurate record of facts relating to society in the form of censuses, sample surveys, etc. When these are specially collected or processed for the purpose of scientific research, the cost should be attributed

R&D covers both formal R&D in R&D units and informal or occasional R&D in other units. Although R&D activities take place throughout the economy, they are often perceived as a whole for science policy purposes, *i.e.* as the "national R&D effort". One aim of the *Frascati* Manual is therefore to establish specifications for R&D input data that can both be collected from a wide range of performers and also be aggregated to meaningful national totals.

Table 1.1.
Gross domestic expenditure on R&D (GERD), 2010

	Per capita, at current PPP$	As a % of GDP	% Financed by		
			Industry	Government	Abroad
Austria	1103.30	2.76	44.3	38.9	16.4
Belgium	749.26	1.99	..	..	..
Canada	702.75	1.80	46.8	..	6.8
Czech Republic	394.76	1.56	48.9	39.9	10.4
Denmark	1228.99	3.06	60.3	27.7	8.8
Estonia	330.85	1.62	43.4	44.3	11.5
Finland	1414.91	3.87	66.1	25.7	6.9
France	770.89	2.26	51.0	39.7	7.3
Germany	1054.46	2.82	..	..	..
Hungary	238.28	1.16	47.4	39.3	12.4
Ireland	725.24	1.79	..	..	..
Italy	401.36	1.26	..	..	..
Korea	1088.19	3.74	71.8	26.7	0.2
Luxembourg	1408.16	1.63	65.9	29.7	4.3
Netherlands	771.87	1.83	..	..	..
Norway	970.01	1.69	..	..	..
Poland	146.33	0.74	24.4	60.9	11.8
Portugal	404.67	1.59	..	..	..
Slovak Republic	147.29	0.63	35.1	49.6	14.7
Slovenia	567.16	2.11	58.4	35.3	6.0
Spain	442.48	1.37	..	..	..
Sweden	1336.70	3.43	..	..	..
Turkey	131.54	0.84	45.1	30.8	0.8
United Kingdom	629.42	1.77	45.1	32.1	16.4
EU-27	608.05	1.91	..	..	..
EU-15	721.20	2.06	..	..	..
Romania	68.86	0.47	32.3	54.4	11.1
Russian Federation	231.39	1.16	25.5	70.3	3.5

Source: Main Science and Technology Indicators, OECD, Paris, 2012.
Note: In the table only countries reporting data for 2010 are shown. Readers interested in other countries can see their figures for other years directly in the MSTI database.

Table 1.1 shows data of Gross domestic expenditure on R&D (GERD), which by definition is total intramural expenditure on R&D performed in the national territory during a given period. OECD supplies data on R&D respecting to its member countries and other seven countries including BRIC (Brazil, Russian Federation, India and China), as well as some figures for aggregates of countries.

The main disadvantage of expressing R&D input series in monetary terms is that they are affected by differences in price levels between countries and over time. It can be shown that current exchange rates often do not reflect the balance of R&D prices between countries and that in times of high inflation general price indices do not accurately reflect trends in the cost of performing R&D. Given the exchange rate failure in take in account the real effort on R&D, the comparisons between countries must use purchasing power parities (PPP).

So, looking at the first numerical column of table 1.1 one can see that the amount of current PPP dollars a country spent per capita on R&D activities, in 2010. These data show significant differences between countries. For instance, while Romania spent 68.86 dollars PPP per capita, Finland spent roughly 20 times more (1414.91 PPP$ per head). If we look to the next column of Table 1.1, we see the expenditure on R&D divided by the GDP in percent terms. This is the most common measure of R&D intensity. As in the first column, the picture is one of great dispersion the percents ranging from 0.47 of Romania to 3.87 of Finland, with an average of 2.06 for the 15 countries that constituted the Euro Area in 2010.

R&D is an activity involving significant transfer of resources among units, organizations and sectors and especially between government and other performers. It is important for science policy advisors and analysts to know who finances R&D and who performs it. So, table 1.1 also shows figures for the share of GERD financed by Government, by industry and by abroad. In this respect it is apparent from the table that the share financed by the industry is considerably higher than the share financed by the government[3]. Exceptions to this pattern are apparent for countries with lower GDP per capita as is the case of Poland, Russian Federation, Romania and Slovak Republic.

a) Functional classification

According to the functions performed by the research units R&D is classified in three types: basic research, applied research and experimental development, as explained below.

1. ***Basic research*** is theoretical or experimental work undertaken primarily to acquire new knowledge of the underlying foundations of phenomena and observable facts, without any particular application or use in view. It analyses properties, structures and relationships with a view to formulating and testing hypotheses, theories or laws. Usually, the results of basic research are not generally sold but are published in scientific journals or circulated to interested colleagues. In basic research, scientists have some freedom to set their own goals. Such research is usually performed in the higher education sector but also to some extent in the government sector. Basic research can be oriented or directed towards some broad fields of general interest, with the explicit goal of enabling a broad range of applications in the future. One example is the public research programs on nanotechnology, which several countries have decided on, but which firms in the private sector may also undertake, with a view to preparing for the next generation of technology. Research on fuel cell technology is a case in point. Such research is basic according to the above definition, as it does not have a *particular* use in view. It is defined in the *Frascati Manual* as "oriented basic research".

---

[3] For the OECD as a whole the share of R&D financed by the industry has been on average approximately double of the one financed by government.

20

2. *Applied research* gives operational form to ideas. It is also original investigation undertaken in order to acquire new knowledge. However, it is directed primarily towards a specific practical aim or objective. The knowledge or information derived from it is often patented but may be kept secret. The results of applied research are intended primarily to be valid for a single or limited number of products, operations, methods or systems. Applied research is undertaken either to determine possible uses for the findings of basic research or to determine new methods or ways of achieving specific and predetermined objectives. It involves considering the available knowledge and its extension in order to solve particular problems. In the business enterprise sector, the distinction between basic and applied research is often marked by the creation of a new project to explore promising results of a basic research program.

3. *Experimental development* corresponds to systematic work, drawing on existing knowledge gained from research and/or practical experience, which is directed to producing new materials, products or devices, to installing new processes, systems and services, or to improving substantially those already produced or installed. In the social sciences, experimental development may be defined as the process of translating knowledge gained through research into operational programs, including demonstration projects undertaken for testing and evaluation purposes. The category has little or no meaning for the humanities.

There are many conceptual and operational problems associated with these categories. They seem to imply a sequence and a separation which rarely exist in reality. The three types of R&D may sometimes be carried out in the same center by essentially the same staff. Moreover, there may be movement in both directions. When an R&D project is at the applied research/experimental development stage, for example, some funds may have to be spent on additional experimental or theoretical work in order to acquire more knowledge of the underlying foundations of relevant phenomena before further progress can be made. Moreover, some research projects may genuinely overlap categories. For instance, study of the variables affecting the educational attainment of children drawn from different social and ethnic groups may involve both basic and applied research.

Box 1.1.
Criteria for distinguishing between types of R&D

Basic research, applied research and experimental development:

– Theoretical investigation of the factors determining regional variations in economic growth is basic research; however, such investigation performed for the purpose of developing government policy is applied research. The development of operational models, based upon laws revealed through research and aimed at modifying regional disparities, is experimental development.

– Analysis of the environmental determinants of learning ability is basic research. Analysis of the environmental determinants of learning ability for the purpose of evaluating education programs designed to compensate for environmental handicaps is applied research. The development of means of determining which educational program to use for particular classes of children is experimental development.

– The development of new risk theories is basic research. Investigation of new types of insurance contracts to cover new market risks is applied research. Investigation of new types of savings instruments is applied research. Development of a new method to manage an investment fund is experimental development.

– The study of a previously unknown language to establish its structure and grammar is basic research. Analysis of regional or other variations in the use of a language to determine the influence of geographical or social variables on the development of a language is applied research. No meaningful examples of experimental development have been found in the humanities.

Pure basic research and oriented basic research:

Oriented basic research may be distinguished from pure basic research as follows: while the pure basic research is carried out for the advancement of knowledge, without seeking long-term economic or social benefits or without making any effort to apply the results to practical problems or to transfer the results to sectors responsible for their application; oriented basic research is carried out with the expectation that it will produce a broad base of knowledge likely to form the basis of the solution to recognized or expected, current or future problems or possibilities.

The examples of box 1.1 illustrate general differences between basic and applied research and experimental development in the social sciences and humanities as well as the distinction between "pure" and "oriented" basic research. Often oriented basic research is identified with "strategic research", a broad notion often referred to in policymaking.

b) Institutional classification

From an institutional point of view statistics distinguish between four sectors of R&D:

1. *The business enterprise sector* that covers all firms (including public enterprises), and organizations whose primary activity is the market production of goods or services (other than higher education) for sale to the general public at an economically significant price. The private non-profit organizations mainly serving them are also included.
2. *The Government sector* groups all departments, offices and other bodies which supply but normally do not sell to the community those common services, other than higher education, which cannot otherwise be conveniently and economically provided, as well as those that administer the state and the economic and social policy of the community. This sector also includes non-profit organizations controlled and mainly financed by government, but not administered by the higher education sector.
3. *Private non-profit sector* where private non-profit organizations serving households (*i.e.* the general public) are included.
4. *Higher education sector*, which covers all universities, colleges of technology and other organizations of post-secondary education, whatever their source of finance or legal status. It also includes all research institutes, experimental stations and clinics operating under the direct control of (either administered by or associated with) higher education institutions.

Table 1.2.
R&D performed by the Business Enterprise sector: BERD and
researchers, 2010

	BERD as a % of GERD	BERD as a % of GDP	BERD as % of value added in industry	Researchers (FTE) per thousand employment in industry
Austria	68.1	1.88	2.87	7.2
Belgium	66.3	1.32	2.20	5.7
Canada	50.7	0.91	1.33	..
Czech Republic	62.0	0.97	1.39	3.0
Denmark	68.1	2.08	3.66	11.5
Estonia	50.0	0.81	1.31	3.0
Finland	69.6	2.69	4.67	13.6
France	61.2	1.38	2.37	..
Germany	67.3	1.90	3.10	6.3
Hungary	59.8	0.69	1.10	3.3
Ireland	68.1	1.22	1.81	5.8
Italy	53.6	0.67	1.12	2.3
Korea	74.8	2.80	4.17	10.1
Luxembourg	70.9	1.16	1.66	4.8
Netherlands	47.3	0.87	1.38	4.1
Norway	51.3	0.87	1.31	7.6
Poland	26.6	0.20	0.28	0.9
Portugal	45.5	0.72	1.25	2.6
Slovak Republic	42.1	0.27	0.37	1.1
Slovenia	67.8	1.43	2.20	4.4
Spain	51.5	0.71	1.04	3.1
Sweden	68.7	2.35	3.98	10.0
Turkey	42.5	0.36	0.52	1.3
United Kingdom	60.9	1.08	1.66	3.5
EU-27	60.8	1.16	1.85	4.2
EU-15	61.8	1.27	2.05	5.0
Romania	38.3	0.18	0.25	..
Russian Federation	60.5	0.70	0.98	4.0

Source: Main Science and Technology Indicators, OECD, Paris, 2012.

Table 1.3.
Higher education and government expenditure on R&D, 2010

	HERD as a percentage of GDP	Percentage of GERD performed by the Higher Education sector	Percentage of GERD performed by the Government sector
Austria	0.72	26.1	5.3
Belgium	0.46	23.3	9.4
Canada	0.69	38.2	10.5
Czech Republic	0.28	18.0	19.4
Denmark	0.90	29.4	2.1
Estonia	0.62	38.1	10.6
Finland	0.79	20.4	9.2
France	0.48	21.3	16.4
Germany	0.51	18.0	14.7
Hungary	0.23	19.9	18.5
Ireland	0.51	28.6	3.3
Israel	0.58	13.2	3.9
Italy	0.36	29.0	14.3
Korea	0.40	10.8	12.7
Luxembourg	0.19	11.4	17.7
Netherlands	0.75	40.8	11.9
Norway	0.55	32.3	16.4
Poland	0.27	37.2	35.9
Portugal	0.59	37.0	7.2
Slovak Republic	0.17	27.6	30.0
Slovenia	0.29	13.9	18.2
Spain	0.39	28.3	20.1
Sweden	0.90	26.3	4.9
Turkey	0.39	46.0	11.4
United Kingdom	0.48	27.2	9.4
EU-27	0.47	24.4	13.7
EU-15	0.50	24.3	12.8
Romania	0.12	24.5	36.8
Russian Federation	0.10	8.4	31.0

Source: OECD, Main Science and Technology Indicators, January 2012.

1.2.2.2. Human resources devoted to R&D

Over the past hundred years we have gained better statistics, in terms of diversity, quality and robustness, thanks to national statistical offices. However, we have also lost some fundamentals. The very first measurements on science were centered on counting "men of science". Today, the statistics on human resources in science and technology are poorer than the ones of expenditures on R&D. National as well as international organizations are aware of this fact, and are trying to remedy the deficiency. But progress is slow.

All persons employed directly on R&D should be counted, as well as those providing direct services such as R&D managers, administrators, and clerical staff. Persons providing an indirect service, such as canteen and security staff, should be excluded, even though their wages and salaries are included as an overhead cost when measuring expenditure. When measuring, R&D Personnel notice has to be taken of the increased use of on-site consultants as well as the outsourcing of R&D to other units or firms. With the greater use of consultants, human resources devoted to R&D may be underestimated when it is difficult to determine whether consultants are on site or part of an outsourcing arrangement. In the case of outsourcing, consultant costs clearly fall under extramural expenditures.

a) *Categories of R&D personnel*

Two approaches may be used to classify R&D personnel: the most commonly used is by occupation; the other is by level of formal qualification.

Box 1.2. ***Classification of the R&D personnel***	
Researchers	Researchers are professionals engaged in the conception or creation of new knowledge, products, processes, methods and systems and also in the management of the projects concerned. Managers and administrators engaged in the planning and management of the scientific and technical aspects of a researcher's work also fall into this category. Their rank is usually equal or superior to that of persons directly employed as researchers and they are often former or part-time researchers. Professional titles may vary from institution to institution, from sector to sector and from country to country. Postgraduate students at the PhD level engaged in R&D should be considered as researchers. They typically hold basic university degrees and perform research while working towards the PhD. Where they are not a separate category and are treated as technicians as well as researchers, this may cause inconsistencies in the researcher series.
Technicians and equivalent staff	Technicians and equivalent staff are persons whose main tasks require technical knowledge and experience in one or more fields of engineering, physical and life sciences or social sciences and humanities. They participate in R&D by performing scientific and technical tasks involving the application of concepts and operational methods, normally under the supervision of researchers. Equivalent staff performs the corresponding R&D tasks under the supervision of researchers in the social sciences and humanities. Their tasks include: – Carrying out bibliographic searches and selecting relevant material from archives and libraries. – Preparing computer programs. – Carrying out experiments, tests and analyses. – Preparing materials and equipment for experiments, tests and analyses. – Recording measurements, making calculations and preparing charts and graphs. – Carrying out statistical surveys and interviews.
Other supporting staff	Other supporting staff includes skilled and unskilled craftsmen, secretarial and clerical staff participating in R&D projects or directly associated with such projects. Other R&D supporting staff are essentially found in ISCO-88 Major Groups 4, "Clerks"; 6, "Skilled Agricultural and Fishery Workers"; and 8, "Plant and Machine Operators and Assemblers".

While both classifications are perfectly reasonable and linked to two different UN classifications – the International Standard Classification of Occupations (ISCO) (ILO, 1990) and the International Standard Classification of Education (ISCED) (UNESCO, 1997) – the differences between them lead to problems of international comparability.

Both occupation and qualification series are important in the broader context of studying human resources in science and technology, because each approach has advantages and disadvantages. However, occupation series reflect the present use of resources and thus are more useful for R&D analysis more strictly defined. Furthermore, they are probably easier for employers to provide and allow for comparisons with other employment series of enterprises and R&D institutes[4]. The occupations described in Box 1.2 are especially designed for R&D surveys.

b) Full-time equivalence (FTE) data

While data series measuring the total number of R&D staff, and notably researchers, have many important uses, they are not a substitute for series based on the number of full-time equivalent staff. The latter is a true measure of the volume of R&D and must be maintained by all OECD countries for international comparisons (see table 1.4).

---

[4] The relevance of qualification series is more apparent for broader analyses, as is the case of setting up total personnel databases and for foreseeing needs and supplies of highly qualified S&T personnel although they may create problems for international comparisons, owing to differences in the levels and structures of national educational systems.

Table 1.4.
R&D personnel and researchers, 2010

	Total R&D personnel (FTE) per thousand labor force	Total researchers (FTE) per thousand labor force	Higher Education researchers (FTE) as a % of national total
Austria	13.7	8.4	32.5
Belgium	12.1	7.7	45.2
Czech Republic	9.9	5.5	34.6
Denmark	18.3	12.2	35.5
Estonia	7.6	5.9	53.6
Finland	20.8	15.4	32.7
Germany	13.2	7.9	27.4
Hungary	7.4	5.0	28.3
Ireland	9.5	6.7	42.3
Italy	8.8	4.2	41.1
Korea	13.5	10.7	14.9
Luxembourg	13.0	6.8	20.4
Netherlands	11.0	5.9	38.8
Norway	13.9	10.2	35.7
Poland	4.6	3.7	60.7
Portugal	9.4	8.2	62.8
Slovak Republic	6.7	5.6	67.2
Slovenia	12.4	7.4	29.4
Spain	9.6	5.8	48.0
Sweden	15.6	9.9	34.4
Turkey	3.2	2.5	51.2
United Kingdom	10.2	7.5	60.6
EU-27	10.4	6.5	41.1
EU-15	11.6	7.2	40.1
Romania	2.6	2.0	41.7
Russian Fed.	11.1	5.9	19.1

Source: OECD, Main Science and Technology Indicators, January 2012.

In fact, there are many different situations. R&D may be the primary function of some persons (*e.g.* workers in an R&D laboratory) or it may be a secondary function (*e.g.* members of a design and testing establishment). It may also be a significant part-time activity (*e.g.* university teachers or postgraduate students). To count only persons whose primary function is R&D would result in an underestimate of the effort devoted to R&D; to do a headcount of everyone spending some time on R&D would lead to an overestimate. The number of persons engaged in R&D must, therefore, be expressed in full-time equivalents on R&D activities.

One FTE may be thought of as one person-year. Thus, a person who normally spends 30% of his/her time on R&D and the rest on other activities (such as teaching, university administration and student counseling) should be considered as 0.3 FTE. Similarly, if a full-time R&D worker is employed at an R&D unit for only six months, this results in an FTE of 0.5. Since the normal working day (period) may differ from sector to sector and even from institution to institution, it is not meaningful to express FTE in person-hours. Personnel should be measured as the number of person-years on R&D over the same period as the expenditure series.

1.2.3. Output indicators

1.2.3.1. Bibliometrics

Bibliometrics is the generic term for data on publications. Originally, it was limited to collecting data on numbers of scientific articles and other publications, classified by author and/or by institution, field of science, country, etc., in order to construct simple "productivity" indicators for academic research. Subsequently, more sophisticated and multidimensional techniques based on citations in articles (and more recently also in patents) were developed. The resulting citation indexes and co-citation analyses are used both to obtain more sensitive measures of research quality and to trace the development of fields of science and of networks.

Bibliometric analysis uses data on numbers and authors of scientific publications and on articles and the citations therein (as well as the citations in patents) to measure the "output" of individuals/research teams, institutions and countries, to identify national and international networks, and to map the development of new (multidisciplinary) fields of science and technology.

Most bibliometric data come from commercial companies or professional societies. The main general source is the set of Science Citation Index (SCI) databases created by the Institute for Scientific Information (United States), which Computer Horizons, Inc., has used to develop several major databases of science indicators. Bibliometric data can also be derived from other, more specialized databases[5].

The propensity to publish varies between fields of science. The utility of bibliometric indicators is greatest for the medical sciences and certain natural sciences. The databases are biased towards articles in English, which may affect international comparisons. Bibliometric methods have essentially been developed by university groups and by private consultancy firms. There are currently no official international guidelines for the collection of such data or for their use as science and technology indicators. In 1989-90, the OECD commissioned a report on the "state of the art" in bibliometrics, which was published in 1997 as an STI working paper (Okubo, 1997).

1.2.3.2. Patent statistics

A patent is a legal property right over an invention, which is granted by national patent offices. A patent provides to its owner a monopoly (with limited duration) for exploiting the patented invention, as a counterpart for disclosure (which is intended to allow a broader social use of the discovery).

---

[5] Although OECD regularly uses bibliometric data in its analytical reports, it does not carry out basic data collection.

Patent documents contain a rich source of information on the invention that is unavailable elsewhere and therefore constitutes a significant complement to the traditional sources of information for measuring diffusion of technological/scientific information (see section on bibliometrics). Patent documents contain information on: *i)* technical features (such as list of claims, technical classification, list of cited patents, etc.); *ii)* history of the application (such as priority date, date of publication, date of filing in the country concerned, date of grant, etc.); and *iii)* information about the inventor (such as name and address of inventors, country of residence, name of applicants, etc.).

Among the few available indicators of technology output, patent-based indicators are probably the most frequently used[6]. Patent-based indicators provide a measure of the output of a country's innovative activity: its inventions. In fact, the scientific literature on the determinants and impact of innovative activity increasingly uses patent data at aggregate (national) or firm level, because of the widely recognized close relationship between patents and innovative output. Patent data are also used to identify changes in the structure and evolution of inventive activity in countries, industries, companies and technologies by recording changes in technology dependency, diffusion and penetration.

The number of patents granted to a given firm or country may reflect its technological dynamism, and the examination of the technologies patented can give some hints on the directions of technological change. However, the drawbacks of patents as indicators are well known. Many innovations do not correspond to a patented invention; many patents correspond to invention with a near zero technological and economic value, whereas a few of them have very high value; many patents may never lead to innovation.

---

[6] The OECD patent manual (OECD, 1994b) outlines the general guidelines for the use and interpretation of patent data as indicators of S&T.

A patent may be granted to a firm, an individual or a public body by a patent office. An application for a patent has to meet certain requirements: the invention must be novel, involve a (non-obvious) inventive step and be capable of industrial application. A patent is valid in a given country for a limited period (usually 17 or 20 years). For purposes of international comparison, statistics on patent applications are preferable to statistics on patents granted because of the lag between application date and grant date, which may be up to ten years in certain countries.

National (INPI, in Portugal; USPTO, in the US) and international (*e.g.* European Patent Office – EPO; World Intellectual Property Organization – WIPO) patent offices are the primary data sources. The OECD assembles, stocks and publishes various patent-based indicators for its member countries in the *Main Science and Technology Indicators* and the *OECD Science, Technology and Industry Scoreboard*.

Patent indicators based on simple counts of patents filed at an intellectual property office are influenced by various sources of bias, such as weaknesses in international comparability (home advantage for patent applications) or high heterogeneity in patent values within a single office. Furthermore, differences in patent regulations across countries make it very difficult to compare patent statistics between two (or more) patent offices.

To overcome the problems associated with the traditional patent indicators (described above), the OECD has been working towards developing a new type of patent-based indicator: patent family counts. A patent family is defined as a set of patents taken in various countries to protect a single invention (characterized by a first application in a country – called the priority application – which has been extended to other offices). The advantages of using indicators based on patent families for statistical purposes are twofold: they improve international comparability by eliminating home advantage and geographical influence; patents included in the patent family are of high value.

Table 1.5.
Patent activity, priority year 2009

	Triadic patent families		Patent applications filed under the PCT		
	Total	Share of countries	Total	In the ICT sector	Biotechnology sector
Australia	289	0.62	1797	489	166
Austria	396	0.85	1221	251	64
Belgium	394	0.85	1089	236	120
Canada	622	1.34	2615	962	232
Czech Republic	22	0.05	174	30	10
Denmark	301	0.65	1060	222	122
Estonia	10	0.02	46	23	3
Finland	335	0.72	1450	640	48
France	2379	5.10	6842	1910	488
Germany	5585	11.98	16414	3637	616
Greece	12	0.03	100	18	5
Hungary	42	0.09	220	59	14
Iceland	5	0.01	35	4	6
Ireland	74	0.16	366	133	29
Israel	362	0.78	1615	626	121
Italy	710	1.52	3015	516	155
Japan	12995	27.88	27044	11294	1063
Korea	1993	4.28	8287	3457	356
Luxembourg	23	0.05	51	7	1
Mexico	12	0.03	144	17	7
Netherlands	873	1.87	3143	1057	237
New Zealand	46	0.10	316	65	32
Norway	116	0.25	726	174	35
Poland	24	0.05	242	59	13
Portugal	27	0.06	125	30	13
Slovak Republic	3	0.01	33	7	1
Slovenia	14	0.03	125	17	8
Spain	234	0.50	1582	342	162
Sweden	872	1.87	2783	1014	115
Switzerland	878	1.88	2117	461	133
Turkey	25	0.05	439	66	3
United Kingdom	1601	3.44	5387	1566	359
United States	13827	29.67	41223	14276	3856
EU-27	13946	29.92	45586	11803	2593
EU-15	13816	29.64	44628	11580	2533
Argentina	8	0.02	44	7	5
China	687	1.47	10476	4551	290
Romania	2	0.01	35	13	1
Russian Federation	63	0.13	771	180	40
Singapore	106	0.23	568	257	83
South Africa	27	0.06	276	39	15

Source: OECD, Main Science and Technology Indicators, January 2012.

Table 1.5 shows data on triadic patent families and on patent applications filed under the PCT (Patent Cooperation Treaty), including the patent counts for two technological areas: the ICT and the biotechnology sectors. According to the OECD definition of triadic patent families, a patent is a member of the triadic patent families if and only if it is filed at the European Patent Office (EPO), the Japan Patent Office (JPO) and is granted by the US Patent and Trademark Office (USPTO). For each country the figures of triadic patents are significantly lower than the ones of the total applications filed under the PCT showing that the former are more valuable than the latter.

Apart from the column representing the share of countries in triadic patent families, all the other columns have a limited role in cross country comparisons, because the different dimension of the countries. For instance, respecting to the inventive capacity we cannot compare the 24 patent families of Poland with the 23 of Luxemburg because the dimension of both countries is very different. If we want to compare the inventive capacity of different countries we must use a relative measure as, for example, the number of patents per capita, instead of the total number of patents[7].

There are other drawbacks associated with using patent indicators for the measurement of technology output and/or innovative activity. Many inventions are not patented because they are protected by other means, such as copyright, trade secrecy, etc. The propensity to patent varies across countries and across industries, and this makes cross-country or cross-industry comparisons difficult[8]. The distribution of the value of patents is skewed, as many patents have no industrial application, hence are of little value, whereas a relatively few are of

---

[7] In cross-country comparisons the number of patents per capita is the most frequently used measure. However, many other (relative) measures can be used. For instance, number of patents per 1000 labor force, number of patents per total exports, number of patents over GDP.

[8] Although it is always affected by the special characteristics of patents, the increasing role of international patent organizations contributes to creating greater comparability of the patent data available for individual countries.

substantial value. Given such heterogeneity, patent counts that assume all patents to be of generally equal value are misleading. However, such biases are minimized if the series of patent counts have a normal distribution, which is likely to happen if we are dealing with large numbers of patents.

1.2.3.3. High-technology products and industries

Although they are the most used, bibliometrics and patent statistics are not the sole output indicators. In the context of the knowledge-based economy, it is helpful to identify those activities and products that are most technology-intensive, using criteria that allow for constructing special internationally harmonized classifications.

In recent years, the OECD has developed technology classifications both by industry, which has generated much interest and widespread application in member countries, and by product. In the industry approach, manufacturing industries are allocated to one of four groups: "high", "medium-high", "medium-low" or "low" technology (see Box 1.3).

A product approach has the advantage of allowing more detailed analysis and identification of the technology content of products. Not all products in a "high-technology industry" necessarily have high technology content; likewise, a high degree of technological sophistication may be found in products from industries with lower technology intensities. However some deficiencies remain. At present, the classifications do not take into account products and industries with low R&D intensities but produced with high-technology machinery and equipment. The classifications are based on R&D intensities only in a certain number of OECD countries[9].

---

[9] International guidelines do not exist. The OECD approach to measuring high-technology products and industries is presented and discussed in "Revision of the High-technology Sector and Product Classification" (Hatzichronoglou, 1997).

Box 1.3: High-tech classification of manufacturing industries	
Eurostat and OECD use the following breakdown of manufacturing industry according to global technological intensity and based on NACE rev. 1.1 at 3-digit level:	
High-technology	**Medium-high-technology:**
Aerospace (35.3) Pharmaceuticals (24.4); Computers, office machinery (30); Electronics-communications (32); Scientific instruments (33)	Electrical machinery (31); Motor vehicles (34); Chemicals, excluding pharmaceuticals (24, excluding 24.4); Other transport equipment (35.2, 35.4 and 35.5); Non-electrical machinery (29)
Medium-low-technology:	**Low-technology:**
Coke, refined petroleum products and nuclear fuel (23); Rubber and plastic products (25); Non metallic mineral products (26); Shipbuilding (35.1); Basic metals (27); fabricated metal products (28)	Other manufacturing and recycling (36 and 37); Wood, pulp, paper products, printing and publishing (20, 21 and 22); Food, beverages and tobacco (15 and 16); Textile and clothing (17, 18 and 19).

Source: Eurostat, Statistics in Focus, Science and Technology, 4/2005, R&D Statistics, Luxembourg, 2005

Considering also the tradable aspects of technology, the *Main Science and Technology Indicators* supply data on export market shares, total imports and total exports for the high technology industries: Aerospace industry, Electronic industry, Office machinery and computer industry; Pharmaceutical industry and Instruments industry.

When constructed, these indicators measure the technology content of the goods produced and exported by a given industry and country, with a view to explaining their competitive and trade performance in high technology markets, because such markets are usually characterized by rapid growth of world demand, offer higher than average returns to trade and affect the evolution of the structure of industry. Although indicators on trade in high-technology products/industries were originally designed as measures of the "output" or "impact" of R&D, they are now seen as having wider use in the analysis of competitiveness and globalization.

1.2.3.4. The technology balance of payments

The TBP (technology balance of payments) registers the international flow of industrial property and know-how. TBP indicators measure the international diffusion of disembodied technology by reporting all intangible transactions relating to trade in technical knowledge and in services with technology content between partners in different countries. The following operations are included in the TBP: patents (purchases, sales); licenses for patents; know-how (not patented); models and designs; trademarks (including franchising); technical services; finance of industrial R&D outside national territory. The following operations are excluded: commercial, financial, managerial and legal assistance; advertising; insurance; transport; films, recordings, material covered by copyright; design; software.

National TBP data may be collected by means of special surveys, but more often they are assembled from existing records, kept by central banks, exchange control authorities, etc. The OECD has assembled a database of "macro" TBP data for most of its member countries, which covers total transactions (receipts and payments) by partner country from 1970. Data for periods since the late 1980s are published in *Main Science and Technology Indicators* (OECD, biannual) and in the associated CD-ROM. In 2000 a new international database for detailed TBP series broken down by industry, type of operation and geographical area was established.

Table 1.6:
Technology Balance of Payments, 2010

	Million of current dollars			Payments as a percentage of GERD
	Receipts	Payments	Balance	
Austria	7075.1	4509.7	2565.4	43.2
Belgium	10939.7	9285.5	1654.2	99.5
Czech Republic	2101.7	2512.6	-410.9	81.3
Denmark	6356.1	5573.5	782.5	58.4
Estonia	473.7	191.6	282.1	62.3
Finland	9517.2	7716.6	1800.6	83.6
Germany	55382.1	45841.0	9541.2	49.6
Greece	715.2	1383.9	-668.7	..
Hungary	3052.5	3645.7	-593.2	244.4
Iceland	279.1	179.1	100.0	..
Ireland	41025.4	44577.5	-3552.1	1203.7
Italy	9821.7	15774.7	-5953.0	61.0
Luxembourg	1527.1	1834.3	-307.3	210.6
New Zealand	636.4	998.2	-361.8	..
Norway	6929.0	3351.7	3577.3	47.4
Poland	3317.6	5459.2	-2141.6	158.0
Portugal	1514.9	1545.9	-31.0	42.5
Sweden	17931.9	9077.6	8854.3	57.8
Switzerland	17808.8	20013.2	-2204.4	..
United Kingdom	43677.3	24083.0	19594.3	60.4
Romania	19.9	75.6	-55.7	10.0
Russian Federation	627.8	1410.1	-782.3	8.2

Source: OECD, Main Science and Technology Indicators, January 2012.

However, there are some drawbacks associated to this type of indicators. For many countries the data are available only at a rather aggregate level. The available data do not necessarily correspond to the definition of TBP, *i.e.* they may cover more or less than transactions with a technological content. The balance is sometimes affected by non-monetary transactions within multinational firms.

There are difficulties for interpreting the data, and the international comparability of the data may be weak[10].

1.2.4. Other approaches

1.2.4.1. The *Oslo Manual* and Innovation statistics

Besides the output indicators mentioned in the previous sections, it is possible to collect data on the number and nature of actual innovations. Such information is usually obtained by special surveys or collected from other sources, such as the technical press. The *OECD Proposed Guidelines for Collecting and Interpreting Innovation Data – Oslo Manual*[11] defines technological product and process innovations as those implemented in technologically new products and processes and in significant technological improvements in products and processes. An innovation is implemented if it has been introduced in the market (product innovation) or used within a production process (process innovation). Of course, innovation involves a series of scientific, technological, organizational, financial and commercial activities. In the various Community Innovation Surveys (CIS) implemented by Eurostat on the basis of the *Oslo Manual*, various modifications have been made to this definition.

Innovation indicators measure aspects of the industrial innovation process and the resources devoted to innovation activities. They also provide qualitative and quantitative information about the factors that enhance or hinder innovation, the impact of innovation, the

---

[10] In 1990, the OECD issued the "Proposed Standard Method of Compiling and Interpreting Technology Balance of Payments Data – TBP Manual" (OECD, 1990). It is the second in the series of OECD manuals on science and technology indicators.
[11] The initial *Oslo Manual* (OECD, 1992) was prepared jointly by the OECD and the Nordic Fund for Industrial Development (Nordisk Industrifond, Oslo) in 1990 and was officially adopted by the OECD as the third in the "Frascati" family of manuals. This manual was jointly revised with Eurostat in 1997.

performance of the enterprise and the diffusion of innovation. A few countries have also introduced some questions on innovation in other surveys, such as the R&D survey.

National data on innovation activities are generally collected by means of surveys addressed to industrial firms on an informal basis. Most OECD member countries have organized such surveys, and the *Oslo Manual* is based on their experience. The first internationally comparable series of data on innovation was collected under the auspices of the Nordic Industrial Fund. The OECD contributed to the preparation of a list of questions proposed for inclusion in harmonized surveys during the launching of the first CIS (Community Innovation Survey) by the European Union. The experience gained from this survey was used in preparing the second edition of the *Oslo Manual*.

Innovation surveys suffer from some problems of quality owing to unsatisfactory response rates in the case of voluntary surveys and differences in the understanding of the concept of innovation among enterprises. The *ad hoc* nature of national surveys is not satisfactory for users, and in many countries innovation surveys give information on R&D that is not consistent with information from R&D surveys. However, the results of innovation surveys have been increasingly used in addition to other more institutionalized measures, as R&D data and Patent counts, in order to give a more complete idea of the Science, Technology and Innovation performance of the European countries. Is this the case of both the *European Innovation Scoreboard* and its successor the *Innovation Union Scoreboard* (IUS)[12].

---

[12] The IUS report, its annexes and the indicators' database are available at http://www.proinno-europe.eu/metrics.

1.2.4.2. The Innovation Union Scoreboard

The Innovation Union Scoreboard (IUS) follows the evolution in innovation inside and outside the EU over time aiming to help the implementation of the Europe 2020 Innovation Union flagship by providing both a comparative assessment of the innovation performance of the EU27 Member States and the relative strengths and weaknesses of their research and innovation systems.The IUS includes innovation indicators and trend analyses for the EU27 Member States, as well as for some EU candidates and other European countries. This is the case of Croatia, Iceland, the Former Yugoslav Republic of Macedonia, Norway, Serbia, Switzerland and Turkey. It also includes comparisons based on a more reduced set of indicators between the EU27 and 10 global competitors (US, Japan, China, etc.).

Box 1.4.
IUS 2011: types of indicators and innovation dimensions
The IUS 2011 uses a total 25 different indicators, grouped in 3 main types of indicators and 8 innovation dimensions (see Figure 1.4). The 3 groups are: • The **Enablers,** which capture the main drivers of innovation performance external to the firm and cover 3 innovation dimensions: 'Human resources', 'Open, excellent and attractive research systems' as well as 'Finance and support'. • **Firm activities,** for capturing the innovation efforts at the level of the firm, grouped in 3 innovation dimensions: 'Firm investments', 'Linkages & entrepreneurship' and 'Intellectual assets'. • **Outputs,** which cover the effects of firms' innovation activities in 2 innovation dimensions: 'Innovators' and 'Economic effects'.

Source: UNU-MERIT (2012).

The IUS intends to use 25 indicators in order to make a composite indicator for representing the innovation performance of national research and innovation systems considered as a whole.

However, the current composite indicator only consists of 24 individual indicators since the last indicator on "High-growth innovative enterprises as a percentage of all enterprises" is not yet completely developed.

Figure 1.4.
The IUS structure

Summary Innovation Index							
Enablers			Firm activities			Outputs	
Human resources	Open, excellent, attractive research systems	Finance and support	Firm investments	Linkages & entrepreneurship	Intellectual assets	Innovators	Economic effects
New doctorate graduates	International scientific co-publications	R&D expenditure in the public sector	R&D expenditure in the business sector	SMEs innovating in-house	PCT patents applications	SMEs with product or process innovations	Employment in knowledge-intensive activities
Population aged 30-34 with tertiary education	Top 10% most cited scientific publications	Venture capital	Non-R&D innovation expenditure	Innovative SMEs collaborating with others	PCT patent applications in societal challenges	SMEs with marketing or organisational innovations	Medium and high-tech product exports
Youth with at least upper secondary education	Non-EU doctorate students			Public-private co-publications	Community trademarks	High-growth innovative firms	Knowledge-intensive services exports
					Community designs		Sales of new to market and new to firm innovations
							License and patent revenues from abroad

Source: UNU-MERIT (2012)

The IUS 2011 uses the most recent statistics from Eurostat and other international sources wherever possible rather than national sources, in order to improve comparability between countries. The composite indicator that measures the Countries' performance is normalized for ranging from a lowest possible performance of 0 to a maximum possible performance of 1. Comparing the Country's composite indicator with the EU27 average, four groups of countries are defined: leaders, follower, moderate and modest innovators.

Box 1.5. IUS 2011: Groups of EU countries
Based on their average innovation performance, the EU member countries are classified in **four groups:** • **Innovation leaders**: Denmark, Finland, Germany and Sweden, which have a performance well above the EU27 average (above 20% or more than the EU27). • **Innovation followers**: Austria, Belgium, Cyprus, Estonia, France, Ireland, Luxembourg, Netherlands, Slovenia and the UK, which show a performance close to that of the EU27 average (less than 20% above but more than 10% below the EU27 average). • **Moderate innovators**: Czech Republic, Greece, Hungary, Italy, Malta, Poland, Portugal, Slovakia and Spain, with a performance below that of the EU27 average. (less than 10% below but more than 50% below of the EU27). • **Modest innovators**: Bulgaria, Latvia, Lithuania and Romania with a performance well below that of the EU27 average (is below 50% that of the EU27).

Source: UNU-MERIT (2012).

Indicators also show that there is a pattern of innovation performance. Countries at the top of the ranking have several strengths in common: first, all innovation leaders show the key role of business activity and public-private collaboration, as Finland, Sweden, Denmark and Germany, which perform very well in Business R&D expenditures. Second, all European top innovators also do extremely well in the commercialization of their technological knowledge, as demonstrated by their good performance on the indicator License and patent revenues from abroad. Third, all of the innovation leaders have higher than average scores in Public-private co-publications per million people, which suggest good linkages between the science base and enterprises. Fourth, most of the innovation leaders have good indicators in other innovation measures related to firm activities. For instance, Sweden dominates in three out of 8 innovation dimensions: Human resources, Finance and support, and Firm investments.

According to the IUS 2011, the good performance in innovation is a sign of **an unbiased national research and innovation system**, since both the innovation leaders and the innovation followers have the smallest variance in their performance across all the 8 innovation dimensions. On the other hand, the moderate and modest innovators are characterized by an unbalanced research and innovation systems. This is particularly clear in the 'Innovators' dimension with very low shares of SMEs introducing product or process innovations as well as SMEs introducing marketing and organization innovations.

Figure 1.5.
IUS 2011: Convergence in innovation performance

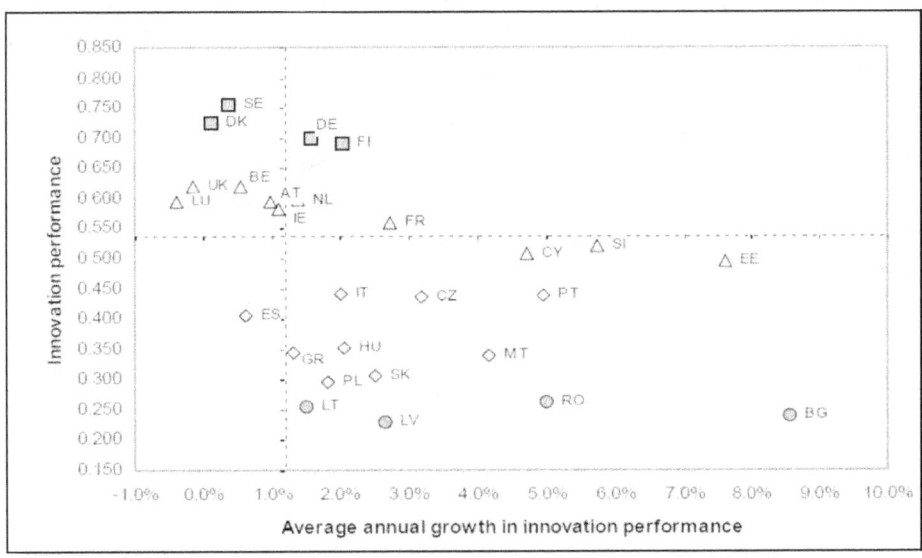

Source: UNU-MERIT (2012), figure 5.

The innovation performance of EU countries, when plotted against their average annual growth rates, shows a steady convergence, given that less innovative Member States have on average been growing faster than the more innovative. In fact, figure 1.5 shows Bulgaria, Estonia, Romania, Portugal and Slovenia as the growth leaders with an average annual growth rate (calculated over a five-year period) well above 5%. However, this convergence process is not generalized. While the Moderate and Modest innovators clearly catch-up to the higher performance level of both the Innovation leaders and Innovation followers, there is no convergence between the different Member States within the Moderate innovators.

A comparison with other European countries not belonging to the European Union shows that Switzerland is the overall Innovation leader continuously outperforming all EU27 countries. Comparing the EU27 with other major global competitors, outside Europe, one sees that the US, Japan and South Korea have a performance lead over the EU27, with the global innovation leaders, US and Japan, mainly dominating the EU27 in indicators capturing business activity and public-private cooperation as for example R&D expenditure in the business sector and PCT patent applications.

The EU27 has a performance lead over Australia, Canada and all BRICS (Brazil, Russia, India, China and South Africa) countries. However, this lead has been decreasing relatively to Brazil and especially to China and India. China has been closing the innovation gap to Europe continuously in the last few years.

Exercises and review questions

1.1. Consider the following set of data:

Indicator	Ireland	Italy	New Zealand	Korea
1. Population (thousands) (2007)	4 339	58 880	4 228	48 456
2. GERD as a % of GDP	1.31	1.13	1.21	3.47
3. BERD as a % of GERD	66.8	48.8	42.7	76.2
4. Researchers per 1000 total employment	6.0	3.6	10.8	9.5
5. Triadic patent families	76	756	50	2 488
6. Exports as a % of imports in "high-tech" industries	231	72	27	182
7. Technology balance of Payments	854.0	118.0	n. d.	-2 941.0

In the sentences presented below, *clearly* indicate the most correct alternative.

1. In Italy, the inventive capacity is higher / approximately equal / lower than the inventive capacity in Ireland.

2. In New Zealand the share of basic research in total R&D is higher / approximately equal / lower than in Italy.

3. In Korea, the R&D intensity is higher / approximately equal / lower than in Ireland.

4. In Korea the exports of disembodied technology are higher / approximately equal / lower than the imports of disembodied technology.

1.2. Consider the following set of data:

Indicator	Denmark	Greece	New Zealand
1. Population (thousands)	5 435	10 950	3 976
2. GERD as a % of GDP	2.43	0.57	1.16
3. BERD as a % of GERD	66.6	30.0	41.8
4. Researchers per 1000 total employment	10.2	4.3	10.5
5. Triadic patent families per million people	42.06	0.99	15.01
6. Exports as a % of imports in high-tech industries	106	23	26

Write a comment upon the technological situation of the countries presented on the above table. (maximum, 25 lines).

1.3. "For Schumpeter, the concept of innovation is not restricted to the technological domain". Do you agree? Justify your answer. (maximum, 15 lines).

Chapter 2

INNOVATION AND ECONOMIC DYNAMICS

Summary
Innovation, economic growth and structural change.
Capitalism as a creative destruction process.
Innovation, long cycles and techno-economic paradigms.
Innovation, diffusion and long waves.
The "technologic gap" model.

2.1. Innovation, economic growth and structural change

The promises of achieving high output without significant adds to conventional inputs, capital and labor, has profoundly influenced policy decisions and expenditure patterns all over the world. Additionally, according to Schumpeter, careful accumulation of capital over the years together with the growth of the labor force is not the essence of economic development. In fact, almost a century ago, Schumpeter wrote in a seminal work that "development consists primarily in employing existing resources in a different way, in doing new things with them, irrespective of whether those resources increase or not"[13].

---

[13] Joseph Schumpeter, *The Theory of Economic Development*, Oxford University Press, New York, 1961. p. 68 (first published in 1911).

However, the spontaneous nature of development must be understood with care. Although the impatience with the slowness of saving and capital accumulation combined with the apparent marvels of modern applied technology tends to persuade us that innovation holds the key to faster economic advance, both in rich countries and especially in poor ones, we must recognize that part of such attraction is mere wishful thinking, the victory of expectations against the common reality of no free lunches.

An essential idea of classical development economics was that economic growth is intrinsically linked to changes in the structure of production. According to this view, industrialization is the driver of technical change, and overall productivity increases are mainly the result of the reallocation of labor from low to high-productivity activities[14]. The traditional view that capital accumulation is important for growth still holds, although losing some ground. The structure of investment is also important, not only because industrialization requires more investment in the manufacturing sector, but also owing to the fact that important investments in financial and business services are needed to support industrial development.

Productivity growth in developed countries mainly relies on technological innovation. For developing countries, however, growth and development are much less about pushing the technology frontier and much more about changing the structure of production towards activities with higher levels of productivity. This kind of structural change can be achieved largely by adopting and adapting existing technologies, substituting imports and entering into world markets for manufacturing goods and services, and through rapid accumulation of physical and human capital. A few developing countries have been able to undertake original research and development in some fields,

---

[14] Early empirical studies had already showed the importance of industrial development for higher long-term economic growth, indicating that it has indeed been an observed "regularity" in development patterns (Kuznets, 1966; Chenery and Taylor, 1968; and Chenery, 1979).

but technological innovation continues to be highly concentrated in the industrialized world.

These fundamental differences in the nature of the growth process between developed and developing countries remain subject to considerable debate among economists. Among the most important analytical developments in recent decades has been the explicit recognition by the so-called new growth theories of the role of external economies in human capital formation and technological innovation, dynamic economies of scale associated to learning by doing, and institutional factors in the growth process. These new insights have moved away from the more traditional perspective that considered accumulation of capital as the key to economic development. They also held the promise of a better linking of policies to economic growth performance.

On the other hand, economists who follow the tradition of classical development thinking have alleged that economic growth in developing countries is about structural change towards high-productivity sectors and that industrialization plays a key role in that process. According to this view, the development of the modern industrial sector will contribute more in dynamic terms to overall output growth, because of its higher productivity growth which results from increasing returns to scale and gains from innovations and learning by doing. The underemployed labor force of the rural sector, but increasingly also of the urban informal sector, provides a fairly elastic supply of labor that allows this process to take place without facing significant labor supply constraints.

Indeed, as the economy expands, those factors become more important for productivity growth as more resources become available for investment in new technology and for the training of workers. Learning by doing and experience accumulated during the production process by both entrepreneurs and laborers are also essential for productivity growth. In this view, productivity is determined endogenously in expanding production sectors. Learning by doing, innovations and industrial linkages are all factors that influence productivity positively when growth accelerates.

Building upon these foundations, one can develop a broader perspective on structural change and growth. In this view, dynamic structural change involves more than just growth of industry and modern services. It is about the ability to constantly generate new activities as well as about the capacity of the new activities to absorb surplus labor and to promote the integration of production sectors within the domestic economy. In other words, innovation can be the bridge between structural change and growth as the seminal contribution of Schumpeter points out. So, in this chapter, we will begin underlining the pioneer approach of Schumpeter, particularly the conception of capitalism as a creative destruction process. In section 3 we return to the Freeman/Perez taxonomy for the explanation of the long run evolution of economies and cycle nature of such evolution. The chapter ends with the "technology gap" model.

2.2. The pioneer approach of Schumpeter: capitalism as a creative destruction process.

Joseph Schumpeter (1883-1950) was an Austrian economist that gave seminal contributions to several economic areas. In fact, he contributed for advancements in the study of economic development and innovation, publishing a fundamental book titled *The Theory of Economic Development*, in 1911, when such topics were not in the mainstream economics agenda. He also contributed to the study of the cycle nature of economic evolution publishing other renowned work — *Business Cycles,* in 1939, after moving to the US in 1932. Some ideas about innovation and development were updated in another important work — *Capitalism, Socialism and Democracy*, published in 1942. In spite of his important contribution, his ideas were almost forgotten till the 1970s when evolutionary economists — Richard

Nelson and Sidney Winter — began to diffuse the Schumpeterian theories.

Nowadays, the seminal contribution of Joseph Schumpeter to the economics of innovation and technological change is commonly acknowledged. However, in our view, understanding his contribution to these issues, as well as why his ideas were forgotten during so much time, calls for an analysis of the conditions of their appearence, dominated by the theory of equilibrium. The theory of general equilibrium let the essential question of economic development open because this theory supposes productive techniques and consumer preferences to be immutable. In these conditions, the economic system only can evolve towards a "steady state" where the only possible increase is quantitative in nature and results from the eventual increment of population and consequent increase in supply of labor.

However, according to Schumpeter, the development process results from successive disequilibria induced by innovation. In his *Theory of Economic Development* he characterizes development as a "spontaneous and discontinuous change in the channels of the circular flow, disturbance of equilibrium, which forever alters and displaces the equilibrium state previously existing"[15]. These ideas had scarce possibilities of constituting the main concern of neoclassical mainstream economics. However, this does not signify Schumpeter is disregard for the importance of the Walrasian equilibrium.

In fact, the first requirement to understand Schumpeter's theory is that he considers the Walrasian equilibrium as a starting point to his theory of development. On the one hand, Schumpeter considers the Walras System indispensable to highlight the fundamental relationships of an economic system and, on the other hand, he thinks that it is not possible to understand the process of development if one does not think about the way this process is born from the rupture of the state of equilibrium.

---

[15] Schumpeter (1961, p. 64)

However, to understand the Schumpeterian theory of development we need to emphasize one of the characteristics of the Walrasian equilibrium: the fact that it is always a process of repetition of the same things, both in terms of production and in terms of consumption. Once competition has driven the system to the position of maximum benefit, a repeated continuous configuration is attained, in a cycle that is always identical to itself. In these conditions, the management of a firm is reduced to a mere routine. Each firm must always produce the same type and the same amount of goods, combining always in the same way the factors needed to their production.

For Schumpeter, the rupture of this stationary world and consequently the beginning of a development process occurs precisely in the sphere of production as a consequence of innovations[16]. These are facts that decisively and deeply alter the old productive systems. Schumpeter classified innovations in five main types (new good, new process, new market, new source of supply, new organization), as we have previously seen in chapter 1.

The dissimilarity between the equilibrium analysis and the Schumpeterian approach becomes perfectly visible, when we look at his definition of innovation. For Schumpeter, economic progress, i.e., what he calls innovation, means essentially putting productive resources to uses till then inexperienced in practice, and retreating them from the uses they have served so far. What matters for the study of this subject is merely the essentially discontinuous character of this process, which does not lend itself to description in terms of a theory of equilibrium. Innovation, as distinct from invention, is not only endogenous but the intrinsic element of the capitalistic economy. Innovation cannot be regarded as an external economy, because this is

---

[16] Schumpeter stresses that equilibrium analysis cannot consider the role of technological change: "Innovations in productive and commercial methods, in the widest sense of the term – including specialization and the introduction of production on a different scale (...) – obviously alter the data of the static system ..." (Schumpeter, 1928:18).

the distinctive feature of the competitive process, as his concept of creative destruction shows and as we will see later.

For the new combinations to be carried into effect, Schumpeter emphasizes first the role of the entrepreneur as the central change-maker. Schumpeter calls "entrepreneur act" to the introduction of an innovation in the economic system and "entrepreneur" to the person that carries out this act. According to Schumpeter, enterprise and entrepreneur are specific facts of development and are non-existent in the stationary state, where the direction of production only implies a routine activity indistinguishable from any other type of work. Entrepreneurs are described as individuals that see the possibility for creating new combinations. They are strongly motivated, more often by the joy of creating rather than by the quest for profit, and they are the driving force for their ability to convince others to support and contribute to the development of the idea. However, in his later contributions Schumpeter stressed the role of technological cumulativeness as the key to innovation and put less emphasis on the role of the individual entrepreneur (Schumpeter, 1942).

The distinction between entrepreneur and mere director of a firm is fundamental, even if it be the same person, or the same team to performs both functions. The decisive difference between the two functions can be illustrated by the difference between the introduction of a new process for producing a woolen cloth and the decision of buying the quantity of wool needed to produce the amount of cloth for the development of a given production process.

The aim of the entrepreneurial activity is profit. The most obvious example of profitable innovation is the production of commonly used goods for a reduced amount of the unitary cost that is paid to the other firms, because the innovator uses a new method that allows to obtain one unit of product from a lesser quantity of a given factor, or of all the production factors. In this case, the entrepreneur will buy the needed inputs at the same prices that the other firms do and will sell its goods to the current price, which is the same price that the other established firms use. Its gains are therefore higher than its costs, and profit consists of this difference.

Two other types of innovation (new organization of production and the discovery of a new cheaper source of the supply of productive resources) are profitable in the same way as the above-mentioned innovation. When innovation consists of the introduction of a new good which presents an increased satisfaction of consumer needs relatively to the one of current production, the possibility of profit arises from the fact that the higher level of satisfaction allows the entrepreneur to ask for a higher price, which surpasses costs, relatively to the price of old goods. In the case of the discovery of new markets or when new goods are created which satisfies needs previously not satisfied, at the beginning prices have no connection with costs and potential buyers are disposed to pay a price higher than the cost.

In the stationary state, as there are no innovations, there is no profit. Although profit is a typical phenomenon of development, which is condemned to disappear with it, development reconstructs continuously the conditions of its reappearance. Since profit appears in a point of the system, the condition that originates it, i.e., innovation, begins its diffusion and when this generalizes, the competitive process that relates prices with costs will imply the disappearance of profit. However profit vanishing is only apparent from the point of view of the firm because actually profit, far from disappearing, extends to all the economic system, where it has determined an increase in wealth, in the same amount of the production effort.

From the viewpoint of the firm, if the innovation process does not stop, profit always reappears. Naturally, it is always possible and it often happens, that the competitive mechanism does not perfectly work. In this case profit, or a part of it, is not diffused all over the economic system and tends to remain within the firm. In this case it loses the nature of profit, as it is not the result of innovative acts and only exists because of routine actions, being therefore more exactly classified as a monopoly rent.

According to Schumpeter, an innovation is usually associated to new organizations, or to a transformation in old organizations. These conditions do not happen in the case of incremental innovations, which do not characterize the development process. The creation of new organizations can occur either as the constitution of new firms or as enlargement of the old ones. In this point, Schumpeter distinguishes between two phases (usually called phase 1 and phase 2, or Schumpeter mark I and Schumpeter mark II, respectively) of organization in the history of capitalism: capitalism of competition and capitalism of big corporations.

The first phase is characterized by the predominance of small and medium firms. The introduction of innovations generally implies the creation of new firms. On the contrary, in the second stage the dominant form is the large corporation which is capable of feeding the innovation process without the need of creation of new firms that compete with the incumbent ones. In this second phase the identification of the entrepreneur is not an easy operation, because no one is a single entrepreneur.

Schumpeter stresses that in the period of competitive capitalism it is usually the owner of firm that develop the entrepreneurial function. In the stage dominated by big corporations the entrepreneurial function can be developed by those who control the corporation or by the responsible ones for the direction of the firm, or even by mere workers. In the second phase entrepreneurial function can be done by a single individual or by a collective entity. In the case of familial firms, those who have developed the entrepreneurial activity also receive the profit. In the industrial system based on big corporations, on the contrary, the profit belongs to the firm and its distribution is a problem that must be solved by the policy of the firm: it can be received by the shareholders, by the administration or even partly by the employees of the firm, therefore without any connection with those who had realized innovative actions. Despite the problem of who receives the profit, according to Schumpeter, the profit is not in any case the compensation for risk, as supported by many other economists. The risk is experienced by the capital owner and not by the entrepreneur.

Another problem addressed by Schumpeter is the financing of innovation. In the stationary state each firm finances its own operations using the current revenue. But the entrepreneur, who must build the organization in which the innovation is materialized, needs a new acquisitive power, which allows him to put under his control the productive resources deviated from the old uses and directed to the new ones required by the innovation. This need for new means of financing is realized by credit, considered by Schumpeter as another fundamental characteristic of economic development. In the same way as in a centrally planned economy the realization of an innovative process makes a command that deviates the productive resources from its current employs to the new uses, in a capitalistic economy the credit to entrepreneur also assumes a similar function because it allows him to use a part of the wealth of the system for his own purposes.

In sum, the Schumpeterian approach shows innovation as an essential component of the competitive process. Firms, dissimilar in terms of size, location and efficiency, confront each other in the product market place and are redeployed by the effect of the competitive process. Entry and exit feed the dynamics of the process. In this context each firm is confronted with a continual redefinition of its relative market context and has to face the competitive threat created by firms that are able to produce at lower costs either because of the access to cheaper production factors or due to more effective production technologies. The duration of the adjustment process to an eventual equilibrium is endless, and firms experience prolonged out-of-equilibrium conditions in which they can earn temporary and yet diverse levels of profits.

Another crucial issue for economic theory separates Schumpeter from the equilibrium theory of Walras and Marshall: the concepts of competition and monopoly. In the equilibrium theory, competition is defined in merely static terms, that is, as the form of market that consists of a numerous amount of firms, all of them producing an identical good, and so small relatively to the total extension of market, that they cannot have, per se, any type of influence on price. It is clear that such structure is not easily found in reality and consequently there are lots of criticisms about this concept. However the Schumpeterian criticism is different from all the others because it is situated at a dynamic point of view.

According to Schumpeter, the true existent competition in a capitalistic economy is not the one between small firms that produce the same good, but the one that innovative firms (where there is entrepreneurial activity) exert in confrontation with the others; it is not competition between identical goods all produced in the same way, but the competition that new goods make to the old ones. This competition process is the basis of "creative destruction", an expression coined by Schumpeter. This means that effective competition is given by the effects that innovations exert on the existing firms.

This competition concept is associated to a different (from traditional) conception of monopoly. The first thing to be noted is the fact that the introduction of an innovation surely implies a certain degree of monopoly: in fact, before its diffusion the innovation is a monopoly of the entrepreneur and the profit that he gains is precisely due to this monopoly. It is not an absolute monopoly, as the one considered in traditional theory, defined in static terms but, on the contrary, a temporary monopoly which in normal conditions is condemned to disappear during the dynamic process of competition. Obviously it can occur that some firms can run away from this competition process; in this case as their gains assume the characteristics of a rent their position in the market is near the traditional monopoly with a permanent character. And it is obvious that this hypothesis was verified often in the history of capitalism.

However, Schumpeter advises to the danger of taking the so-called "monopolistic practices" as a symptom of a structure disease that forcedly retards the pace of development. In this respect, his argumentation encompasses two main points. Firstly, because the big corporation, where the monopoly is more frequent, is often the location where innovations are more favored, due to more capacity to finance research and experimental development. Secondly, the suspending of competition, even in a more or less long period of time, it is only a warranty against the risk derived from innovations of large dimension, a risk that could be unbearable in conditions of a quickly mutable market. Furthermore, covering the cost of innovation also requires other actions directed at stabilization of the market like patents, trade secrets, etc.

The transition between phase 1 and phase 2, that is, the shift from the stage where innovations are usually incorporated in new firms to the stage where innovations are concretized within the firms already existent, does not imply, according to Schumpeter, either a decrease in the intensity of economic development, or a decrease in its quality, but on the contrary, it is possible to say that there is an acceleration with the transition from phase 1 to phase 2. Schumpeter rejects the thesis that capitalism is destined to disappear in a final crisis owing to reasons inherent to its economic mechanism. Although Schumpeter was convinced that "is impossible to survive to capitalism", this conviction is based on extra-economic considerations.

According to Schumpeter capitalist economic development, which is generated by innovative processes, does not evolve in a continuous and uniform way, but in contrast, it advances through a periodical succession of cycles. Business cycle is not an accessory aspect of capitalism, but the very way where development is manifested in this economy, as it was previously asserted by Marx.

For Schumpeter, the basis for the appearance of a cyclic process consists of the fact that innovations are not uniformly distributed along time but on the contrary, they have a propensity to pile up during some periods. This is evidence given by the history of the capitalist system, which he explains considering that the introduction of an innovation requires the rupture of a large amount of social resistance (that is usually opposed to all that is presented as essentially new and different from the routine practices) and whose defeat is turned easier when someone with an superior entrepreneurial character, has opened the route for struggle with those traditional lines.

On the other hand, the excess of innovations determined in this way is destined soon or later to exhaustion, because along time the amount of new goods that result of the same innovations makes more and more impact on the market. Additionally the increasing pace of the reimbursement of financial charges by entrepreneurs causes inflation, which decreases the prospects of profit and diminishes the pace of innovations. This mechanism is, for Schumpeter, the crucial factor responsible for the cyclical evolution of development.

It is also important to mention that for Schumpeter the period of time between the adoption of an innovation and the moment when the innovation begins to give results in form of goods that come to the market varies according to the nature of the innovation. This is the origin of cycles with different periodicity. In this respect, Schumpeter distinguishes between three types of business cycles: the first type corresponds the so-called long waves (Kondratieff cycles), which have a variable period between 54 and 60 years. The first goes from 1783 to 1842, the second from 1842 to 1897 and the third was the existent one when Schumpeter wrote his book dedicated to the theoretical, statistical and historical analysis of business cycles. The second type is constituted by cycles that have 9 to 10 years (Juglar cycles), a Kondratieff cycle being formed by 6 Juglar cycles. The third type consists of Kitchin cycles (with 40 months long). This means that each Juglar cycle encompasses 3 Kitchin cycles.

It is worth noting that, the unequal distribution of innovations along time can be an effect rather than a cause of business cycles, and in this case it acts as a magnifying element of cyclical fluctuations. So, the contribution of Schumpeter in this area needs to be integrated in a more general theory of fluctuations, which includes the contribution of Keynes and some post-Keynesian authors. However, the important point to stress now is Schumpeter's central idea, which argues that in the capitalistic system, economic development has an unavoidably cyclical nature.

2.3. Innovation, long cycles and techno-economic paradigms

In Chapter 1 we have introduced the Freeman and Perez taxonomy of innovations. As we have seen, the fourth type of that taxonomy of technical change, the most complex, is called changes in 'techno-economic paradigm'. Such changes have a major influence on the behaviour of the entire economy, and so they can be called 'technological revolutions'. A change of this kind carries with it many clusters of radical and incremental innovations, and may eventually embody a number of new technology systems. A crucial characteristic of this fourth type of technical change is that it has persistent effects throughout the economy, i.e., it not only leads to the emergence of a new range of products, services, systems and industries in its own right; it also affects directly or indirectly almost every other branch of the economy.

2.3.1. Characteristics of techno-economic paradigms

According to Freeman and Perez, each techno-economic paradigm generates a phase of sustainable economic growth. The decline of one paradigm (which corresponds to the emergence of a new paradigm) is associated to a slow growth period.

A new paradigm emerges in a world still dominated by an old paradigm and begins to demonstrate its comparative advantages at first only in one or a few sectors. A new techno-economic paradigm develops initially within the old, showing its decisive advantages during the 'downswing' phase of the previous Kondratieff cycle. Each paradigm has a diffusion pattern: it always begins in a small number of industries and from these it is spread to a much wider range of industries. However, it becomes established as a dominant technological regime only after a crisis of structural adjustment, involving deep social and institutional changes, as well as the replacement of the motive branches of the economy.

Each paradigm is associated to a specific 'key factor'. The key factor is clearly perceived as one that presents a set of characteristics that make it appropriated to a generalized adoption. Because it presents low and rapidly falling relative cost, and (at least apparently at the moment of the paradigm emergence) an almost unlimited availability of supply over long periods, it has a clear potential for the use in many products and processes throughout the economic system. There is a specific key input associated to each paradigm. For instance, coal was associated to the second, steel to the third, energy (particularly, oil) to the fourth and the "chips" (microelectronics) to the fifth. In sum, the key factor is an input with unlimited availability, with decreasing costs and, above all, with potential to be incorporated in all economic sectors.

The new paradigm emerges in a context dominated by the old one and only substitutes it when it demonstrates comparative advantages in all sectors. The fastest-growing new sectors are thus not those which are the motive branches of an established, technological regime. There is no possibility for a new paradigm to displace an old one until it has first clearly demonstrated such advantages and until the supply of the new key factor or factors already satisfies three conditions: falling costs, rapidly increasing supply, and pervasive applications. Thus a period of rapid growth in the supply of the key factor(s) occurs already before the new paradigm is established as the dominant one, and continues when it is the prevailing regime.

A new techno-economic paradigm emerges only gradually as a new 'ideal type' of productive organization to take full advantage of the key factor(s) which are becoming more and more visible in the relative cost structure. The new paradigm discloses the potential for a quantum jump in total factor productivity and opens up an unprecedented range of new investment opportunities. It is for these reasons that it brings about a radical shift in engineering and managerial 'common sense' and that it tends to diffuse as rapidly as conditions allow, replacing the investment pattern of the old paradigm.

Until the present time, Freeman has identified five techno-economic paradigms. In figure 2.1, which gives a stylized view of those paradigms, it is visible that each paradigm generates a phase of sustainable economic growth. It is also apparent that the decline of one paradigm (which corresponds to the emergence of a new paradigm) is associated to a slow growth period.

Figure 2.1.
The five techno-economic paradigms identified by Freeman and Perez

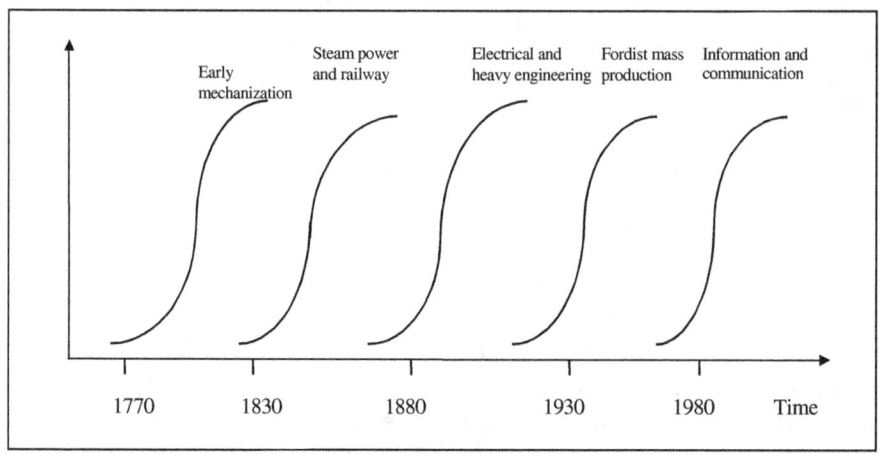

Table 2.1 presents a synthesis of the main characteristics of each of the five paradigms identified by Freeman and Perez in what respects to periods, type of innovations, key factors and economic organization.

Table 2.1.
Main characteristics of the five paradigms

Period	Innovations	Key-sectors	Economic organization
1770s -1840s	Early mechanization	Textiles, channels, roads	Small firms, individual entrepreneurs, local capital.
1830s – 1890s	Steam power and railways	Steam engines, railways, maritime transport	Large dimension emergence; Big corporations
1880s – 1940s	Electricity and heavy engineering	Electric engineering, Chemical processes, Steel shipbuilding,	Giant firms cartels and trusts; merges; anti-trust laws
1930s – 1980s	fordist mass production	Motor vehicles, aeronautics, durable goods, synthetic's material	Oligopolies, multinationals, FDI, vertical integration
1970's – …..	Information and communication technologies	Computers, software, telecommunications, digital technologies	Networks of big and small firms, Technology based firms, clusters.

Let's see a synthetic characterization of two paradigms: the fordist mass production and the information and communication technologies paradigms. With reference to the former, the technological regime, which predominated in the post-war boom, was one based on low-cost oil and energy-intensive materials (especially petrochemicals and synthetics). The fordist paradigm was led by giant oil, chemical, automobile, and other mass durable goods producers. Its 'ideal' type of productive organization at the plant level was the continuous-flow assembly-line turning out massive quantities of identical units. The 'ideal' type of firm was the 'corporation' with a separate and complex hierarchical managerial and administrative structure, including in-house R&D and operating in oligopolistic markets in which advertising and marketing activities played a major role. It required large numbers of middle-range skills in both the blue-

and white-collar areas, leading to a characteristic pattern of occupations and income distribution.

The massive expansion of the market for consumer durables was facilitated by this pattern, as well as by social changes and adaptation of the financial system, which permitted the growth of several types of consumer credit. Additionally, the paradigm required a vast infrastructural network of motorways, service stations, airports, oil and petrol distribution systems, which was promoted by public investment on a large scale already in the 1930s, but more massively in the post-war period. At various times in different countries both civil and military expenditures of governments played a very important part in stimulating aggregate demand for motor vehicles, and petroleum products.

On the other hand, with the arrival of the Information and communication technologies paradigm, based on a cheap microelectronics widely available, with prices expected to fall still further and with related new developments in computers and telecommunication, it is no longer "common sense" to continue along the (now expensive) path of energy and materials-intensive inflexible mass production. The 'ideal' information-intensive productive organization increasingly links design, management, production and marketing into one integrated system, which allow firms to produce a flexible and rapidly changing mix of products and services adaptable to market niches and even to individual costumers.

These characteristics have impact in non-economic aspects such as types of urbanization and new ways of organizing labor. The flexible production systems, and the call for new ways of organization and networks, leave behind the continuous-flow assembly-line and, consequently, the need of concentrate huge quantities of workers in large industrial cities. On the other hand, the information intensive key input allows not only for customization but also for work from home.

2.3.2. Some additional thoughts about innovation and long business cycles

The idea that the dynamics of economic evolution in the capitalistic social order is not of a simple and linear nature but rather of a complex and cyclical character is nowadays generally recognized. In fact, the dynamics of the capitalist economies over long historical periods shows that they experience significant long-term variations in their aggregate performance. However, the economic science has not succeeded in explaining the nature and the types of these cyclical, wave-like movements. As Rosenberg and Frischtak puts it "The question is whether these long-term variations are more than the outcome of a summation of random events, and further, whether they exhibit recurrent temporal regularities that are sufficiently well-behaved to call them long waves."

The sequence of techno-economic paradigms identified by Freeman and Perez brings the possible association of techno-economic paradigms and long waves to mind . However, such association calls for answers to some questions: if these paradigms are in any way associated to the existence of long cycles, what is the cause and the consequence? What is the origin of a long cycle? What is the economic logic of long waves? The answers to these questions call for empirical investigation and appropriate theory.

In the empirical front, the first attempt to identify and systematize the long waves was made by Kondratieff. Using data about prices, interest rates, wage rates, trade, industry and consumption, for France, the UK and the US he identified three long waves of an average length of about 50 years. Long cycles, as Kondratieff put it, "...arise out of causes which are inherent in the essence of the capitalist economy" (1979, p. 543). The cyclical behavior of the capitalist economy in turn shapes the conditions that are favorable to technological innovation. In this specific sense, therefore, technological activities stand in the position of dependent variables whose volume and timing are determined by those deeper-rooted forces that shape the rhythm of capitalist development. So, in sum, Kondratieff was convinced that capitalism has its own internal regulating mechanisms, and he regarded the rhythm of the long cycle as an expression of these internal forces. His view is that innovations are structured and have their timing determined by such long-term movements.

On the contrary, Schumpeter is the chief and most prominent author of the opposite view — that long waves are caused by, and are an episode of, the innovation process. In Schumpeter's view, innovation is at the core of both cyclical instability and economic development with the direction of causality moving clearly from fluctuations in innovation to fluctuations in investment and from that instability in investments to cycles in economic development (see figure 2.2).

Figure 2.2.
Direction of causality in the Schumpeterian theory of business cycles

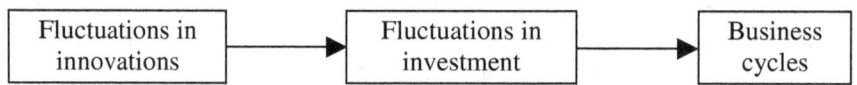

However, determining the direction of causality is only a part of the problem. The important question is: what conditions need to be fulfilled in order for technological innovation to generate long cycles of the periodicity postulated by Kondratieff? This complex question calls for a theory, which might account not only for the presence of long cycles in some real economic variable, but also would have to fulfill a set of logically interdependent conditions: causality, timing, economy wide repercussions and recurrence (Rosenberg and Frischtak, 1984).

2.4. Innovation, diffusion and growth: the Fagerberg's "technology gap" model.

The "technology gap" growth model, developed by Fagerberg (1987, 1988), is a contribution to a better understanding of the impacts of innovation and diffusion on economic growth. According to Jan Fargerberg the rationale of his model is different from the underlying principles of the general equilibrium models (neoclassical models), because the former embodies one of the Schumpeterian chief principles about development: the idea that economic development is the outcome of a succession of disequilibria generated by two forces in confrontation, the innovation and the diffusion or imitation. In fact, the model considers innovation and diffusion as two explaining factors of economic growth, but with different directions. While innovation (the development of new technology) may lead to divergence between firms or nations, imitation tends to erode differences in technological skills, and hence lead to convergence with technological frontier.

In the remainder of this section we will begin by exposing the underlying principles of the model and the hypothesis that Fagerberg tries to test, followed by the adaptation of the model to empirical tests and a synthesis of the main conclusions drawn by Fagerberg and Verspagen (2002) founded in model empirical applications.

2.4.1. Rationale

Fagerberg justifies the technology-gap theory of economic growth as an application of Schumpeter's dynamic theory of economic development, developed for a closed economy, to a world economy characterized by competing national economies. So, he analyses economic development as a disequilibrium process characterized by the interplay of two conflicting forces: Innovation, which tends to increase economic and technological differences between countries, and imitation or diffusion that tends to reduce them.

When a country behind the world innovation frontier succeeds in reducing the productivity gap vis-à-vis the frontier countries, that does not depend on its imitative efforts alone, but also on its innovative performance, and on the innovative performance of the frontier countries. Even if a country behind the world innovation frontier succeeds in reducing the productivity gap essentially through imitating activities, it cannot surpass the frontier countries in productivity without overcoming them in innovative activity as well. In general, the outcome of the international process of innovation and diffusion — with regard to the development levels of different countries — is uncertain. The process may generate a pattern where countries follow diverging trends, as well as a pattern where countries converge towards a common mean.

For modeling these ideas, one assumes that the level of production in a country (Y) is a multiplicative function of the level of knowledge diffused to the country from abroad (D), the level of knowledge created in the country (N), the country's capacity for exploiting the benefits of knowledge (C), whether internationally or nationally created, and a constant (Z), as in the following Cobb-Douglas function:

$$Y = ZD^{\alpha}N^{\beta}C^{\delta} \tag{2.1}$$

And where α, β and δ are the respective elasticities.

By differentiating and dividing through with Y, we obtain:

$$y = \alpha d + \beta n + \delta c \tag{2.2}$$

Where y, d, n, and c are the growth rates of the respective variables in equation (2.1).

It is further assumed, as is customary in the diffusion literature, that the diffusion of internationally available knowledge follows a logistic curve. This implies that the contribution of diffusion of internationally available knowledge to economic growth is an increasing function of the distance between the total level of knowledge appropriated in the country and that of the country on the technological frontier (for the frontier country, this contribution will be zero). Let the total amount of knowledge, adjusted for differences in size of countries, in the frontier country and the country under consideration to be T_f and T_i, respectively. Then:

$$d = \mu - \mu \, (T_i/T_f) \tag{2.3}$$

Next, substituting the result of equation (2.3) in equation (2.2), we will have:

$$y = \alpha\mu - \alpha\mu\left(T_i/T_f\right) + \beta n + \delta c \tag{2.4}$$

Accordingly, following this approach, economic growth can be seen as the result of three factors:

1. The diffusion of technology from abroad. The contribution of this factor increases with the distance from the world innovation frontier.
2. The growth in nationally produced knowledge.
3. The growth in the country's capacity for exploiting the benefits offered by available technology, whether created within the country or elsewhere.

2.4.2. Empirical tests and conclusions

In the equations of the preceding section, there are two concepts related to a country's level of economic and technological development, the total level of knowledge appropriated in the country (T_i), and the level of knowledge created within the country (N). The first concept (T_i) refers to the total set of techniques in use in the country, whether invented within the country, or diffused to the country from the international economic environment. T_i cannot be measured directly. What can be measured are the resources associated with the use of these techniques (technology-input-measures), or the output of the process in which these techniques are used (technology-output-measures). As we have seen in Chapter 1, expenditures on R&D (research and development) and employment of scientists and engineers may be mentioned as measures of the technology-input-type. Patent counts may be referred to as an example of the technology-output-measure type.

However, since patents primarily reflect innovative (or inventive) activity, not imitation, patent-based measures give biased estimates of the level of technological development for countries that rely mainly on imitation. Fagerberg has, therefore, chosen to use a productivity-based measure, real GDP per capita, as a proxy for T_i. Since exchange-rates are known to produce downward biased estimates of real GDP per capita for countries with productivity levels well below the world productivity frontier, the conversion from national currencies to US dollars was made using the PPPs (purchasing power parities).

The second concept (N) refers to the national technological activity, i.e., the amount of technology created within the country. It is the domestic technology base as opposed to the use of imported technology. This cannot be measured directly either. The most obvious proxies are R&D and patent counts. To a certain extent R&D reflects both innovation and imitation, since a certain scientific base is a precondition for successful imitation in most areas (Freeman, 1982; Mansfield, 1982), while patents primarily reflect innovation, not imitation. Thus, patents will be preferred to R&D[17].

In order to measure the country's capacity for exploiting the benefits of knowledge (C) Fagerberg used the investment rate (i.e., Investment/GDP averaged over the indicated period). For dependent

---

[17] In the former empirical tests Fagerberg used external patent applications, while in more recent tests he used USPTO patents.

variable, the annual average growth rate of GDP was used. The patent variable is specified as the average annual growth rate of the number of patents adjusted for country dimension, R&D as the average annual growth rate of real R&D expenditures. For testing the robustness of the regressions, Fagerberg includes other control variables (for instance, the shares in GDP of *value added in agriculture, exports* or *manufacturing and services*).

Fagerberg (1987, p. 88) summarized the basic hypotheses of this approach in four points as follows:

1. There is a close relation between a country's economic and technological level of development.

2. The rate of economic growth of a country is positively influenced by the rate of growth in the technological level of the country,

3. It is possible for a country facing a technological gap, i.e., a country on a lower technological level than the countries on 'the world innovation frontier', to increase its rate of economic growth through imitation or 'catching up').

4. The rate at which a country exploits the possibilities offered by the technological gap depends on its ability to mobilize resources for transforming social, institutional and economic structures.

To test the first of these four relationships, we can regress the level of GDP per capita on two different technology indicators: the number of patents per million people, and total R&D expenditures as a fraction of GDP. The hypothesis was that this relation is loglinear rather than linear, because countries closer to the technological frontier depend more on the development of new knowledge than on diffusion. Especially patents must be considered as an indicator of the development of new knowledge, while a part of R&D will generally be related to assimilating foreign technology. Thus, countries with high values of GDP per capita are expected to have relatively higher values of patenting per million people, while this relationship may be somewhat less steep for R&D.

Figure 2.3.
Triadic patent families and level of economic development

$y = 0.0417e^{0.0002x}$
$R^2 = 0.6691$

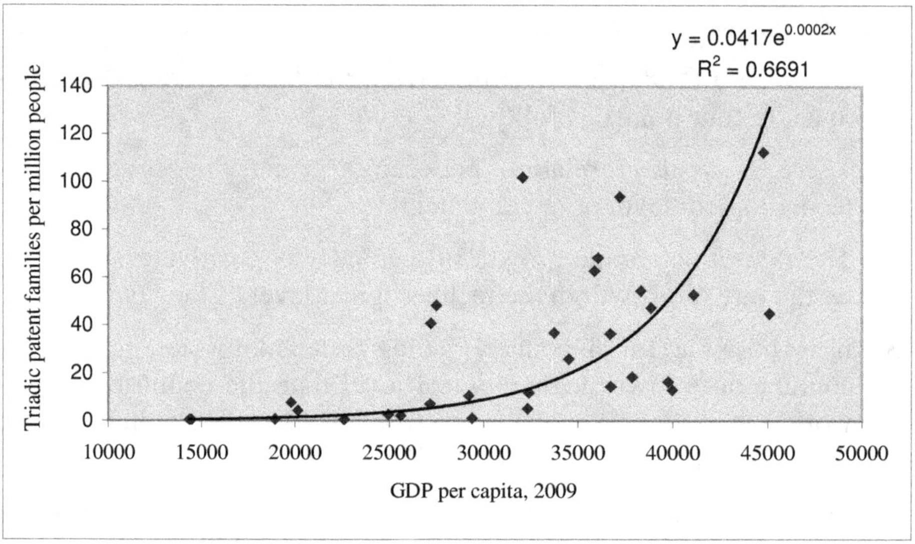

Source: Author calculations based on MSTI (2012) data.

Figure 2.3 shows the relationship between triadic patent families (priority year = 2009) per million people and the level of economic development measured by GDP per capita, in 2009 converted by PPPs (purchasing power parities), for 32 OECD countries (all members of this international organization except Luxembourg and Norway, which are clearly outliers). The positive but non-linear association between the two variables is apparent in figure 2.3. A relation of the same type is also visible when we use the number of PCT patent applications per million people, instead of triadic patent families, as is visible in figure 2.4.

Figure 2.4.
PCT patent applications and level of economic development

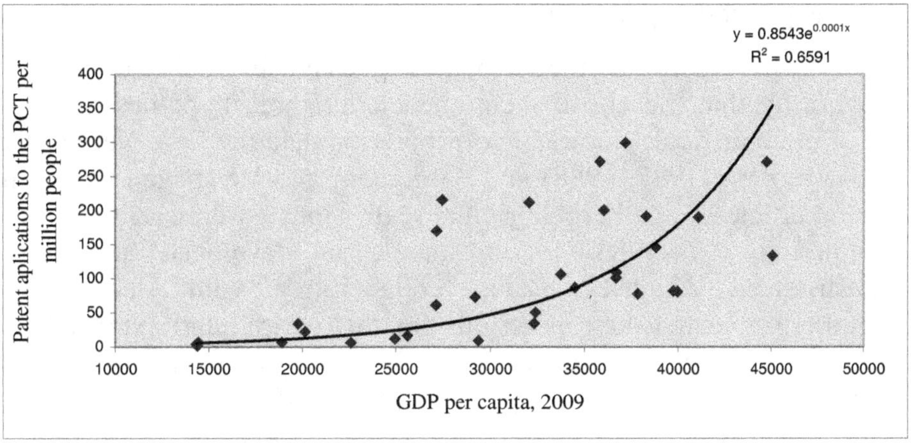

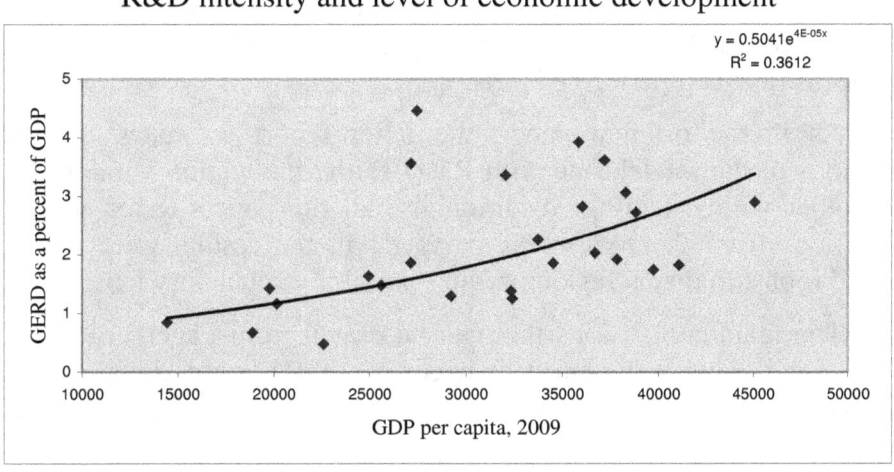

Source: Author calculations based on MSTI (2012) data.

Figure 2.5.
R&D intensity and level of economic development

Source: Author calculations based on MSTI (2012) data.

Figure 2.5 shows the association between the two levels (economic and technological) using R&D intensity (i.e., total expenditure on R&D in percent of GDP). A non-linear positive relationship also results, but now such relationship evolves at a slower pace, as previously predicted.

Let us return to the hypothesis tested by Fagerberg. It is noteworthy that the above mentioned latter three hypothesis, which are of more difficult empirical corroboration than the first, were tested by Fargerberg (1987, 1988) and Fargerberg and Verspagen (2002) in several articles. Fagerberg's original regressions[18] were carried out for the period 1973-1983, for a sample of developed and semi-industrialized countries. Later, collaborating with Verspagen[19], Fagerberg repeated the regressions for this period, and extended the time coverage to an earlier period (1966-1972) as well as two more recent periods (1984-1995 as a whole and 1990-1995 separately). Some slight differences in sample[20] and in the data set compared to Fagerberg's original regressions were introduced. In particular, while the original data on patents were referred to total external patents (patents by the country's residents in foreign countries), the latter paper uses data on patenting in the United States. Also, while original used civil R&D, the latter paper used total R&D (including non-business financed/performed R&D).

As in the original paper, the latter report estimates for two versions of the model, one with R&D as the innovation variable and the other with patenting. Additionally, all the papers tested various equations from the robustness perspective, but results were always found robust to the inclusion of other possible explanatory factors.

The main conclusions that can be drawn from Fagerberg (1987, 1988) and Fagerberg and Verspagen's (2002) regressions are the following:

---

[18] Fagerberg (1987, 1988).

[19] Fagerberg and Verspagen (2002).

[20] Compared to the former, the latter sample excludes India, Mexico, Brazil, Argentina, but adds Malaysia, Philippines, Turkey, Singapore and Thailand.

1. In general, the test confirms the basic hypotheses underlying the model, i.e., that innovation, potential diffusion and other (complementary) factors related to the exploitation of this potential matter for economic growth.

2. There appear to be important differences in the working of the model for the two sets of countries taken into account by the study (as witnessed by the estimates for the DME-dummy). In particular, the catch-up potential seems to be very important for the NICs, while it matters much less for the DMEs, and this to some extent holds for the other conditioning variables, i.e. investment and industrial structure, as well.

3. The importance of innovation for economic growth appears to increase over time. This holds for both R&D- and patents-based measures of innovation, and for NICs as well as DMEs. The impact is especially significant in the most recent period.

4. The opposite holds for the role of manufacturing, which had a higher and more significant impact before 1973 than it is shown to have later.

5. The choice of the innovation variable has only a few implications for the impact of other variables. When R&D is used, the estimated impact of the catch-up potential decreases through time, while this evidence is less clear in the case of patents. 20 Another difference relates to the impact of manufacturing on growth, which is higher and more significant when R&D is used.

Fagerberg and Verspagen concluded in addition that there have been important changes through time in the way innovation-diffusion and economic growth and welfare are correlated. Although the association between economic and technological levels of development is in itself not new, the importance of R&D and innovation for the outcome of economic dynamics has increased. They also concluded that these changes hold not only for the countries at the technology frontier, but for countries in the process of catching up as well.

Exercises and review questions

2.1. The full understanding of the Schumpeter's innovation theory implies concepts different from mainstream definitions of competition and monopoly. Do you agree? Justify your answer.

2.2. Some authors have argued that the world economy is in a transitional phase, from the fordist mass production paradigm to the information technology paradigm. Write a small essay about the alleged transition. Do not forget to characterize those paradigms.

2.3. The technology gap model includes technology variables as explanatory factors of economic growth. What are such variables and what are their effects on the rate of economic growth.

*

*   *

Chapter 3
ECONOMIC FUNDAMENTALS OF INNOVATION

Summary
The modern evolutionism.   The "demand pull" vs. "technology push" controversy.   The induced technological change.   Adoption and diffusion of technologies: The S Curve.

3.1. Introduction

Why does technological change occur? Why do firms innovate? The reason put forward, based on Schumpeter's work, is that firms are seeking profits. A new technological device is a source of some advantage for the innovator. In the case of productivity-enhancing process innovation, the firm gets a cost advantage over its competitors which allows it to gain a higher mark-up at the prevailing market price or, depending on the elasticity of demand, to use a combination of lower price and higher mark-up than its competitors to gain market share and seek further rents. In the case of product innovation, the firm gets a monopoly position due, either to a patent (legal monopoly), or to the delay before competitors can imitate it. This monopoly position allows the firm to set a higher price than would be possible in a competitive market, thereby gaining a rent.

Other works have emphasized the significance of competitive positioning. Firms innovate to defend their competitive position as well as to seek competitive advantage. A firm may take a reactive approach and innovate to prevent losing market share to an innovative competitor. Or it may take a proactive approach to gain a strategic market position relative to its competitors, for example by developing and then trying to enforce higher technical standards for the products it produces.

However, technical change is far from straightforward. New technologies compete with established ones, and in many cases replace them. These processes of *technological diffusion* are often long-lasting, and usually involve incremental improvements both to new and established technologies. In the resulting turbulence, new firms replace incumbents who are less capable of adjusting. Technical change generates a reallocation of resources, including labor, between sectors and between firms. As Schumpeter pointed out, technical change can mean creative destruction. It may also involve mutual advantage and support among competitors or among suppliers, producers and customers.

In sum, for Joseph Schumpeter it seems clear that innovation is the distinctive element of a dynamic process which cannot be analyzed with the equilibrium approach. In his words: "If, then, the putting to new uses of existing resources is what 'progress' fundamentally consists in; if it is the nature of the entrepreneur's function to act as the propelling force of the process; if entrepreneur's profit, credits, and the cycle prove to be essential parts of this mechanism – the writer even believes this to be true of interest – then industrial expansion *per se* is better described as a consequence than a cause; and we should be inclined to turn the other way around what we have termed the received chain of causation" (Schumpeter, 1928, p. 38).

In their seminal book *An Evolutionary Theory of Economic Change* (1982) Richard Nelson and Sidney Winter suggest that theoretical progress should be understood as the interaction between two different levels of theorizing: formal theory and appreciative theory. While the former is described as logical and mathematical, the latter is said to be closer to empirical observation, to the development of which it is assumed to provide both guidance and interpretation. "In a well-working scientific discipline", they argue, "the flow of influence is not only from formal to appreciative theorizing, but in the reverse direction as well. Phenomena identified in applied work that resist analysis with familiar models, and rather causal if perceptive explanations for these, become the grist for the formal theoretical mill. Somewhat informal explanations in the style of appreciative theory are abstracted, sharpened, and made more rigorous" (Nelson and Winter 1982, p. 47). It was Nelson and Winter's view that the mainstream economics neglect of appreciative theorizing was one important reason behind the failure of the discipline to deal with many important real world phenomena.

Arguably, the distinction between formal and appreciative theorizing may also be important for understanding the field of evolutionary economics itself. On the one hand, there is an important body of work on evolutionary modeling, following the initial contributions by Nelson and Winter and others. This work is often inspired by evolutionary biology and draws on mathematical tools that have become popular in biology and other natural sciences.

However, the term evolutionary economics is also often associated with a rather influential approach in economics which stresses the importance of out-of-equilibrium dynamics, even though this tradition is not directly influenced by biological approaches. The economist Joseph Schumpeter is certainly a central contributor to this literature, as are many economic historians such as, for example, Alexander Gerschenkron, Moses Abramovitz and Nathan Rosenberg. What these authors have in common is that they focus on evolution as a process of qualitative change that takes place in historical time, driven by firms, governments and other organizations (rather than individuals) with a diverse set of motivations, decisions rules and capabilities (rather than optimizing behavior and perfect information).

For Joseph Schumpeter, firms introduce technological changes as a competitive instrument to gain market shares and to increase profitability. Profits last as long as imitators enter the market and draw prices closer and closer to marginal costs. Imitative entry pushes the growth of demand. Monopolistic competition characterizes the industrial dynamics in product markets much more than price adjustments in competitive markets. This perspective is also the distinctive feature of the evolutionary school, which emphasizes the role of technological change in shaping structural change and growth (Dosi *et al* 1990), which we will deal with in next section. Next we will present the "demand pull" vs. "technology push" controversy. In section 3 we synthetically present the theories of induced technological change. We will end with the description and interpretation of the adoption/diffusion process, in section 4.

3.1. Evolutionary approach

The evolutionary approach is the result of the collective work of several authors such as: Nelson, Winter, Freeman, Dosi, Bell, Pavitt, Fagerberg, etc. Partly because of the diversity of authors engaged in the evolutionary approach, the term evolutionary has been used in many different ways. So, it is the time to make a clarification of the concept.

One central division in the many different ways in which the term evolutionary economics has been used is that between approaches that take biological metaphors rather strictly, and those that do not. In the first set of contributions, the biological notions of natural selection and (random) genetic mutation are applied to economic processes such as industrial dynamics (Dosi, Marsili *et al.*, 1995) or economic growth (Silverberg and Verspagen, 1998). Silverberg (1988) gives an early overview of the methods and issues in this branch of literature. This leads to a central role of heterogeneity between economic agents (and hence the rejection of the standard neoclassical concept of the representative agent), and to the use of economic selection as a counterpart of natural selection.

A second interpretation of the term 'evolutionary economics' takes the analogy to biology much less strictly. In this case, the term is used to refer to a set of theories, more often informal than formal, which pay particular attention to the role of technology and institutions in the process of economic growth. Usually, these contributions draw inspiration from Schumpeter's (1911) notion of disequilibrium dynamics resulting from the introduction of innovations. Examples of this approach are Fagerberg (1987), Fagerberg (1988), Freeman and Soete (1987) or Dosi, Pavitt and Soete (1990).

As we have seen in the previous chapter, when we dealt with the economic dynamics, the perspective offered by evolutionary theories is one of the world economy as a process of constant transformation. Such dynamics is deeply routed in the microeconomic behavior. Technologies and institutions change in time, and what drives economic growth in one epoch (e.g., economies of scale in relation to mass production) might become much less important, or substituted by a different factor (e.g., network economies) in a different epoch. In terms of economic growth rates, such a process is quite different from the neoclassical notion of steady state growth.

For the evolutionary approach, technological change cannot be treated like the exogenous fall of manna from heaven. Technological change is endogenous to the economic process and it is the main factor of repeated change as it is the result of the pressure of economic forces both on the demand and the supply side. So, technological change cannot be treated like the customary result of usual activities, such as increases in production factors. On the other hand, technological change yields results that are far larger than any rational calculations based upon marginal productivity.

Another main theme in the evolutionary literature of economic growth is that one cannot make a useful distinction between 'economic' and 'non-economic' factors. Authors following this perspective think of the 'social system' as composed of different 'domains', e.g., the techno-economic domain and the socio-institutional domain (Perez, 1983), or the separate domains of technology, economy and institutions (Dosi, 1984). Each of these domains has its own dynamics and explanatory processes, but what is important is that these domains exert strong mutual influences. Examples of such interaction are the impact of culture on regional innovation systems, or the influence of firm organization on economic growth. In this view, any 'model' that limits itself to pure economic factors provides a much too narrow perspective on economic growth.

The need to combine the endogenous understanding of economic dynamics into a homogenous framework by means of which technological and organizational change is introduced in the economic system with the elements of surprise and unknown that necessarily characterize it has always proven difficult for economic analysis. The evolutionary approach provides an effort to go beyond some criticisms made to neoclassical theories by building upon different traditions of analysis: the bounded rationality and limited knowledge framework for understanding individual decision-making, the inducement approach, the economics of learning and the economic analysis of path dependence. The key point here is that firms are induced to change their routines and their technologies in many different circumstances.

The innovative reaction is sometimes made necessary and shaped by path dependence. At the same time it is made possible, and yet constrained, by the dynamics of learning and the effects of limited knowledge and bounded rationality. So, the evolutionary approach provides a framework to analyze technological change as the endogenous and induced outcome of an out-of-equilibrium self-sustaining dynamics that takes place in a set of highly specific and contextual circumstances. To do this, it integrates different strands of literature in order to overcome the criticisms and shortcomings of each of them.

Firms are viewed as learning agents which do not limit the scope of their action to adjusting prices to quantities and vice versa. They are also able to change their technology intentionally and purposely, as well as their strategies (Penrose, 1952). The introduction of innovation, however, is risky and agents are reluctant to innovate. Innovative behavior is requested and induced by emerging discrepancies between plans and reality when performances fall below the expected levels of satisfying thresholds. Complete flexibility in any given condition causes actual losses or results below subjective expectations. The constraints imposed by path-dependence and limited knowledge about alternative techniques in the existing range of options reduce the scope for traditional substitution and make it expensive and resource-consuming. So, when this happens, the search for new routines and new technologies must start.

Firms introduce technological change as a creative response to their expectations about market changes in incentives: hence technological change is generated in out-of-equilibrium conditions. The introduction of new technologies by each agent in turn engenders new discrepancies between the expectations of any other agent and actual market conditions. Hence technological change feeds technological change and out-of-equilibrium conditions further reproduce out-of-equilibrium outcomes.

It is the firm's behavior at a micro level that allows for the existence of rules (firms act according to a set of decision rules and not only aiming to the profit maximization). The universe of firms is not homogeneous, because of imperfect and heterogeneous processes of comprehension and learning. And so, firms differ in many respects, such as: dimension and degree of concentration (market share); technological capacity; technological variety (there are specific paths of technological accumulation); and behavioral diversity. This means that different firms, even facing identical innovation opportunities will follow different investment strategies, different R&D policy, different price policy, etc. Also there is an organizational diversity across firms.

Differently from the neoclassical theory, in the evolutionary approach firms act with imperfect information; additionally, the access to information has a cost, it is not free. Furthermore, part of the knowledge stock is tacit. The tacit knowledge is not easily transferable and so there are many technologies that give some market power to specific firms. Knowledge presents a selective nature and also a cumulative and sequential character: learning capacities are bounded and different from firm to firm. So, there is a variety of learning processes, from formal, as R&D activities, to more informal, as exchange of information between clients and providers, originating a variety of possible solutions. The competitiveness between firms and the collective interaction processes function as selection mechanisms, generating a differentiated growth of different entities.

To sum up, the evolutionary approach is dynamic. This means that in order to conveniently explain economic phenomena, it is not enough to observe its actual state. It is also necessary to consider its trajectory. Evolution is a consequence of processes of learning and innovation on the one hand, and competitiveness and selection, on the other.

3.2. The "demand pull" vs. "technology push" controversy

Has the rate and direction of technological change been more heavily influenced by changes in market demand, or by advances in science and technology? This was the core question of the debate that emerged in the 1960s and 1970s in the US, polarized around "demand pull" and "technology push". One couple of studies, in the 1960s, clearly exposes the enthusiastic dispute between the two views. In Project "HINDSIGHT", the US Department of Defense presented a historical analysis of the importance of "need" in the development of 710 key military innovations, or what they referred to as "Events", for example, satellites, aircraft, and missile systems (Sherwin and Isenson, 1966; Greenberg, 1966). According to Sherwin and Isenson (1967) "nearly 95 percent of all events were motivated by a recognized defense need. Only 0.3 percent came from undirected science". Their explicit conclusion was that defense procurement was critical to innovation.

In reaction, the project "TRACES" (Technology in Retrospect and Critical Events in Science), sponsored by the National Science Foundation, also from the US, identified the role of basic research in 341 "research events," focusing on magnetic ferrites, the video tape recorder, oral contraceptives, the electron microscope, and matrix isolation (IIT, 1968). The study emphasized that the effects of basic research become dominant once a sufficient time frame for analysis is used, i.e. 30 years. Federal budget appropriation considerations may have promoted the adoption of strong positions, but the polarization of the debate was also emblematic of academic debates at the time, which tended to frame the two explanations of technical progress as mutually exclusive.

a) Science and technology-push

The core of the science and technology-push viewpoint is that advances in scientific understanding determine the rate and direction of innovation. Advocates of this view articulated a highly influential version of the well-known "linear model". As we have seen before, this is based on a progression of knowledge from basic science to applied research, to product development, to commercial products. The increasing importance of science in the innovation process, the increasing complexity, which necessitated a long-term view, the apparently strong correlations between R&D and innovative output, and the inherent uncertainty of the innovation process, are arguments that contributed to enforce this view.

A central critique of the technology-push argument is that it ignores prices and other changes in economic conditions that affect the profitability of innovations. Another one is that the emphasis on a unidirectional progression within the stages of the innovation process was incompatible with subsequent work that emphasized feedbacks, interactions, and networks (Kline and Rosenberg, 1986; Freeman, 1994).

Later work offered a less deterministic version of the technology-push argument, while still emphasizing the role of science and technology. For example, some argued that the availability of exploitable "technological opportunities" plays a role in determining the rate and direction of innovation, and that these may depend on the "strength of science" in each industry (Rosenberg, 1974; Nelson and Winter, 1977; Klevorick et al., 1995). Other authors stressed the "capabilities push," the idiosyncratic firm-level competencies and the changes in a firm's ability to pursue particular technology paths (Freeman, 1974). An extension of these ideas is that firms must invest in scientific knowledge to develop their "capacity to absorb" knowledge and exploit opportunities emerging from the state-of-the-art elsewhere (Mowery, 1983; Rosenberg, 1990; Cohen and Levinthal, 1990). Another string raised the issues of the inter-relatedness of the technological system (Frankel, 1955); the importance of flows of knowledge between sectors (Rosenberg, 1994) and that bottlenecks in the system raised "technological imperatives" to be overcome (Rosenberg, 1969). Finally, replies to the critiques of the 'linear' aspect of the model defended the "sequential" character of science and technology-push (Rothwell, 2002).

The concept of science and technology-push that emerged from all the above developments was multi-dimensional and acknowledged some of the nuances of the innovation process that the strictly 'linear' model ignored. It also differed from earlier versions of the concept in that the abandonment of the language of mutual-exclusivity meant that technology-push could be considered a complement to alternative hypotheses, such as demand-pull.

b) Demand-pull

The demand-pull perspective has a long tradition in economics. For Adam Smith, the growth of demand leads to a wider and deeper division of labor. The new levels of the division of labor stimulate the learning processes, the generation of new technological knowledge and hence they offer new opportunities for the introduction of new technologies by profit-seeking entrepreneurs. The demand-pull mechanism works at the aggregate level and provides an indication to understand the rates of introduction of new technologies. Here the relationship between the division of labor and the extent of the market is the founding stone of a process of creation of opportunities. The growth in demand and the increasing levels of division of labor help understanding the rates of technological change.

Studies in the 1950s and 1960s argued that demand drives the rate and direction of innovation. Changes in market conditions create opportunities for firms to invest in innovation to satisfy unmet needs. Demand guides firms to work on certain problems (Rosenberg, 1969). Shifts in relative factor prices (Hicks, 1932); geographic variation in demand (Griliches, 1957); as well as the identification of "latent demand" (Schmookler, 1962, 1966); and potential new markets (Vernon, 1966); all affect the size of the payoff to successful investments in innovation. In the specific case of energy technologies, changes in the prices of conventional sources of energy affect the demand for innovation both within existing processes and for alternative devices.

Critics of the demand-pull argument attacked it on three grounds. Methodologically, the definition of "demand" in empirical studies had been overall considered inconsistent and was therefore regarded as too broad a concept to be useful. A second line of criticism was that demand explains incremental technological change far better than it does discontinuous change, so it fails to account for the most important innovations (Mowery and Rosenberg, 1979). A third point of view addresses the arguments' assumptions concerning firm capabilities, expressing skepticism about: (1) how effectively firms can identify "unrevealed needs" from an almost infinite set of possible human needs, (2) the extent to which firms in general have access to a large enough stock of techniques to address the variety of needs that could be expected to emerge, and (3) how far firms might venture from existing "routines" in order to satisfy unmet demands (Simon, 1959).

In sum, science and technology-push fails to account for market conditions, while demand-pull ignores technological capabilities. Following the critical responses to both arguments, weaker versions of each were used to support the claim that both supply and demand side factors are necessary to explain innovation. But some authors add other arguments: both factors (demand and technology) do not just contribute; they also interact. In a survey of 40 innovations, Freeman (1974) found that successful innovations showed the ability to connect, or "couple" a technical opportunity with a market opportunity. Pavitt (1984) showed that industry specific attributes affect the relative importance of each.

Demand-pull and technology-push are "necessary, but not sufficient, for innovation to result; both must exist simultaneously" (Mowery and Rosenberg, 1979). Similarly, Kleinknecht and Verspagen (1990) found statistical anomalies in the work of Schmookler (1962) that led them to a much weaker estimation of the role of demand; they too emphasized the role of the combination of demand-pull and technology-push. Often, adoption of one technology depends upon complementary innovations and the potential of one may stimulate investment in the other (Mowery and Rosenberg, 1989). Overall, cumulativeness, networks, and feedback effects appear significant.

With all the above criticisms and the highlighting on interactions, the reduction of the innovation process to two causal factors proved limiting, and their use in the literature consequently declined. However, as we will see in chapter 7, these terms continue to be invoked in policy debate over the allocation of public funds to stimulate innovation.

3.3. The induced technological change

According to the induced technological change approach, new technologies are introduced in response to conditions in the factor markets. First, a distinction has to be made between the models of induced technological change, which focus attention on changes in factor prices, and the models of induced technological change, which stress the static conditions of factor markets. In the former approach, following Marx and Hicks, firms are induced to change their technology when the price of a factor of production increases (Hicks, 1932).

The inducement mechanism elaborated by Karl Marx helps understanding the direction of technological change. The dynamic process progressively exhausts the relative availability of production factors. The introduction of technological changes appears to be more profitable if directed towards the reduction in usage of the resources that have become scarcer and towards an increase of the resources that are relatively more abundant. Technological change makes possible to substitute the factors that have become relatively more expensive and to make a more productive use of the resources that are relatively less expensive. The inducement mechanisms engendered by the changing relative prices helps explaining the direction of technological change as well as the rates.

On the other hand, Hicks (1976) clearly characterizes the inducement hypothesis, providing a definition of induced invention: "An induced invention is a change in technique that is made as a consequence of a change in prices". This means, "if the change in prices had not occurred, the change in technique would not have been made".

According to the generalization of the basic hypothesis put forward by Binswanger and Ruttan (1978) and recently updated by Ruttan (1997 and 2001), firms introduce new technologies, which reduce the use of the factor whose costs have increased. A change in factor prices acts as an inducement, and explains both the rate and the direction of the introduction of new technologies. The introduction of new technologies complements and actually increases the standard substitution process, i.e. the technical change involving the selection of new techniques, defined in terms of factor intensities, on the existing isoquants. Inducement concerns both direction and intensity. The stronger, the increase of wages (or any other factor) is; the larger, the effects will be, both in terms of labor saving intensity and in terms of the amount of innovation being introduced.

This approach to the induced technological change differs from the static (macroeconomic) version, elaborated by Kennedy, von Weiszacker and Samuelson, according to which firms introduce new technologies in order to save on the production factors that are relatively more expensive. In this second approach the levels of factor price matter instead of the rates of change. This approach has shown a major limitation of the former. From simple algebraic calculation it is in fact clear that firms have an incentive to introduce labor-intensive technologies, in labor abundant and capital scarce regions and countries, even after an increase in wages. The Kennedy-von Weiszacker-Samuelson approach however is severely limited from the dynamic viewpoint. It is no longer clear when and why firms should innovate. Consistently only the direction of technological change can be induced, rather than the rate (Binswanger and Ruttan, 1978; Ruttan, 1997 and 2001).

The macroeconomic model, however, points out one important thing: i.e. there is a clear incentive to introduce a technology which makes the most intensive use of the resources that are locally most abundant. However, there is a contradiction here between the macroeconomic model and the microeconomic one. In the microeconomic model, firms are induced to introduce new labor saving technologies by an increase of wages. But, on the other hand, in a labor abundant region there is a strong incentive to introduce labor-intensive technologies, rather than labor saving ones, even after an increase in wages.

Both microeconomic and macroeconomic approaches have been often criticized using Salter's argument, according to which firms should be equally ready to introduce any kind of technological change, either labor or capital intensive, provided it makes possible to reduce production costs and increase efficiency.

3.4. Adoption and diffusion of technologies: The S Curve

Diffusion is a slow and a cumulative process. Unlike the invention of a new technology, which often appears to occur as a single event or jump, the diffusion of that technology usually appears as a continuous and rather slow process. Yet it is diffusion rather than invention or innovation that ultimately determines the pace of economic growth and the rate of change of productivity. Until many users adopt a new technology, it may contribute little to our well-being.

Diffusion is a slow process. Why? In general several market imperfections contribute to the slow speed of diffusion. On the one hand there is imperfect information, on the other hand there are hurdles related with the market structure. Both factors increase the uncertainty of the diffusion process. Additionally the need of some complementarities (e.g., qualifications, labor force, etc.) also plays an important role.

There are two stylized facts about the adoption of new technologies: first, adoption is usually an absorbing state, in the sense that we seldom observe a new technology being abandoned in favor of an old one. This is because the decision to adopt faces a large benefit minus cost hurdle; once this hurdle is passed, the costs are sunk and the decision to abandon requires giving up the benefit without regaining the cost. Second, under uncertainty about the benefits of the new technology, there is an option value to waiting before sinking the costs of adoption, which may tend to delay adoption.

The most important thing to observe about the adoption decision is that at any point in time the choice being made is not a choice between adopting and not adopting but a choice between adopting now or deferring the decision until later. Why? Because the nature of the benefits is different from the nature of the costs. As a rule, the benefits from adopting a new technology, as in the wireless communications example, are flow benefits that are received throughout the life of the acquired innovation. However, the costs, especially those of the non-pecuniary "learning" type, are typically incurred at the time of adoption and cannot be recovered.

Figure 3.1.
Diffusion rates in the US for selected Consumer products

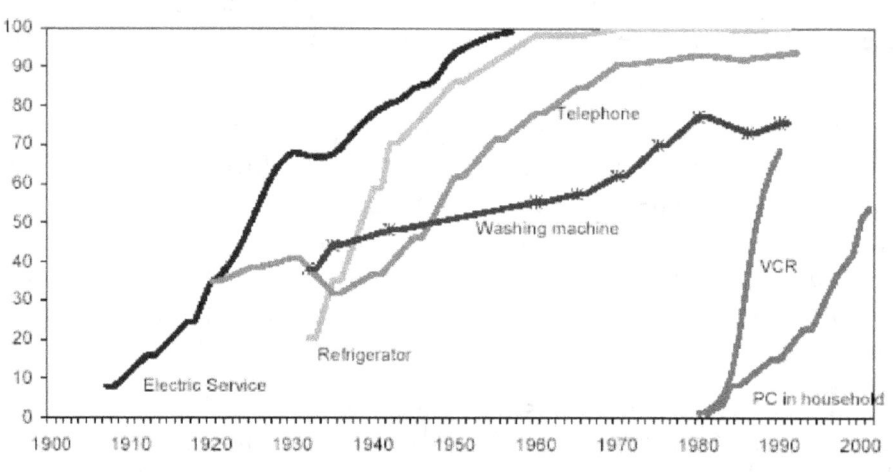

Source: Hall and Khan (2003), figure 1.

Figure 3.1 shows the diffusion rates of several consumer goods in the United States. As is apparent, in spite of the different characteristics of consumer products depicted in the figure, the diffusion follows an S curve: adoption proceeds slowly at first, accelerates as it spreads throughout the potential adopters, and then slows down as the relevant population becomes saturated. Why the S shape? There are several theories that can be summarized in two different mechanisms explaining such shape: one mechanism is based on the adopter heterogeneity, while the other uses the adopter learning to explain the S shape pattern.

The heterogeneity model assumes that different individuals place different values on the innovation. The following set of assumptions will generate an S-curve for adoption: 1) the distribution of values placed on the innovative product by potential adopters is normal (or approximately normal); 2) the cost of the innovative product is constant or declines monotonically over time; 3) individuals adopt the innovative product when the valuation they have for it is greater than the respective cost.

In the learning or epidemic model, consumers can have identical tastes and the cost of the new technology can be constant over time, but not all consumers are informed about the new technology at the same time. Because each consumer learns about the technology from his or her neighbor, as time goes by, more and more people adopt the technology during any period, leading to an increasing rate of adoption. However, eventually the market becomes saturated, and the rate decreases again.

*

*   *

Exercises and review questions

3.1. Following the widespread recognition of the role that technology plays in economic growth and early work characterizing the process of innovation, a debate emerged in the 1960s and 1970s about whether the rate and direction of technological change has been more heavily influenced by changes in market demand or by advances in science and technology. Write a comment upon the above statement. (Do not forget to characterize the mentioned debate and to provide two criticisms for such controversy).

3.2. Has the rate and direction of technological change been more heavily influenced by changes in market demand or by advances in science and technology? This was the core question of the debate that emerged in the 1960s and 1970s in the United States of America. Write a small essay about this topic. (Do not forget to characterize the debate and to present the most important criticisms about such controversy).

3.3. The diffusion of innovations follows an S curve. Do you agree? Justify your answer referring to the different theories that explain the S shape pattern.

Chapter 4

SECTORAL PATTERNS OF INNOVATION

Summary
Innovation, firm size and market structure.
Appropriability, technological opportunities and cumulativeness.
The Pavitt's taxonomy: techno-economic characteristics of sectors.
Dynamics of Pavitt's taxonomy: application to the analyses of
industrialization.

Introduction

One may find that in certain industries innovative activities are concentrated on few major innovators while in others innovative activities are distributed among several firms. In certain industries large firms do the bulk of innovative activities while in others small firms are quite active. Additionally, in some industries new innovators continuously appear while in others only established firms innovate; and so on. So, the ways innovative activities take place may be quite different across industries and across countries. So some questions emerge: are there patterns of innovative activities? What are the most important innovation determinants? While these questions can be seen as different ways of questioning the same thing, we will begin with methodological reasons to answer to the second question.

We can divide the innovation determinants into four groups: i) The characteristics of firms; ii) The techno-economic characteristics of sectors; iii) The territorial determinants of innovation (the geography of innovation); and iv) The institutions, including science policy and technology policy. In the present chapter we will deal basically with firms and industries; chapter 5 will be dedicated to territorial determinants; in chapter 6 we will deal with institutional determinants including the innovation systems (national, regional and local) and finally chapter 7 will conclude with a brief analysis of the technology policy.

4.1. Firm's characteristics

It is important to consider the characteristics of firms because firms are at the center of the innovation process. Firm has a central role to play in innovation because: a) it is inside the firm that the most important technology accumulation is carried out; b) it is inside the firm that innovation is used and tested for its profitability; c) it is inside the firm that incremental innovations appear and their utilization possibilities are tested; d) it is inside the firm that the learning process (learning by doing, learning by using) is carried out.

But, what are the relevant characteristics of firms? The traditional view calls attention basically to dimension and concentration: a U inverted curve was the dominant shape between innovation and these two characteristics. However, this pattern has been defied in empirical grounds. So, in this section we will deal with this traditional view and afterwards presents the other more recent view that calls attention to the possible reverse causality and to the role of appropriability, technological opportunities and cumulativeness played on the dimension and structure of firms[21]. But, the ways innovative activities take place may also be quite different along time, with a consequent different role for dimension and market structure. This is why we will begin by discussing the Schumpeterian patterns of innovative activities.

a) Schumpeterian patterns of innovative activities.

Schumpeter identified two major patterns of innovative activities. The first one, labeled by Nelson and Winter (1982) Schumpeter Mark I, was proposed in *The Theory of Economic Development*. This pattern of innovative activity is characterized as 'creative destruction' with technological ease of entry and a major role played by entrepreneurs and new firms in innovative activities. The second one, labeled Schumpeter Mark II, was proposed in *Capitalism, Socialism and Democracy*. In this work Schumpeter discussed the relevance of the industrial R&D laboratory for technological innovation as well as the key role of large firms. This second pattern of innovative activity is characterized by 'creative accumulation' with the prevalence of large established firms and the presence of relevant barriers to entry for new innovators.

The Schumpeter Mark I regime lays emphasis on the innovating entrepreneur who observes possibilities for the introduction of new products, and subsequently enters in this so-called market niche. By entering this niche, the entrepreneur challenges the incumbent firm and hence the existing leading-edge technology and/or product. This is

---

[21] Apart from these aspects, there are some consensual views. For instance, it is recognized that internal structure and organization matters: a more flexible organization, with good vertical and horizontal flows of information, make innovation more probable. Additionally, labor force qualification also plays an important role. Some empirical studies have shown that labor qualifications condition the innovative capacity of firms, with a likely positive correlation between the two variables.

why this process of quality improving or vertical innovation, which results from (uncertain) research initiatives, is called creative destruction. The notion of creative destruction implies by definition the natural property of new inventions to make the leading-edge technology and/or products obsolete, which more or less forces the incumbent firm to withdraw from the market. The market structure, in a Schumpeter Mark I regime, is characterized by many small firms who use the public domain of existing knowledge or the general and easy accessible knowledge stock to innovate, while the knowledge created by their invention is added to the public domain and used by the next entrepreneur to challenge the incumbent, and so on.

The dealings described above contrast with the Schumpeter Mark II regime. This considers innovative activities conducted by large and established firms. The process of the innovative activities of these firms is often called creative accumulation, because when large firms successfully innovate, they often appropriate the main part of their invention (instead of being forced to add their newly acquired knowledge to the public domain), which leads to a strong positive feedback loop from innovation to increased R&D activities. This self-reinforcing process is mainly due to firms prevent their innovation from imitation and hence appropriate the profits from an innovation to the largest extent possible. In this view, several devices are noteworthy: patents, secrecy, lead times, costs and time required for duplication, learning curve effects, superior sales efforts, and differential technical efficiency due to scale economies.

The Schumpeterian Mark I and Mark II patterns of innovation could also be labeled *widening* and *deepening* regimes. A widening regime of innovative activities is related to an innovative base, which is continuously enlarging through the entry of new innovators, and to the erosion of the competitive and technological advantages of the established firms. A deepening pattern of innovation, on the contrary, is related to the dominance of a few firms which are continuously innovative through the accumulation over time of technological and innovative capabilities (Malerba and Orsenigo, 1995).

Box 4.1.
One or two Schumpeters?

Much attention has been called to the evolution of Schumpeter's thinking about the role of technological change in economic development. A divide between the 'first' and the 'second' Schumpeter has been identified. The first Schumpeter is allegedly based on the tradition of the *Theory of Economic Development* originally published in German in 1911, which draws attention to entrepreneurship as the driving mechanism. Entrepreneurs that create new firms to enter the markets would primarily introduce technological innovations.

The second Schumpeter is based upon the 1942 book *Capitalism, Socialism and Democracy* where the driving role of the large corporation as the engine for the introduction of innovations is highlighted. The well-known Schumpeterian hypothesis is based on this second book: monopolistic power and the large size of corporations favor the allocation of resources to generating new technologies. A split between static and dynamic efficiency arises. But the second Schumpeter also expresses some concern about the long-term viability of the competitive mechanisms based on innovations, because of the increasing routinization of the activities leading to the introduction of innovations within the large corporation. Innovation here is fully endogenous, but only a question of 'routine'.

However, the two Schumpeter's views are not contradictory; they can coexist consistently, as is apparent in the "Instability of Capitalism" published in *The Economic Journal* in 1928. In this article the 'two Schumpeters' are well integrated.

---

b) Innovation, firm size and market structure

Much of the empirical literature about innovation determinants has focused on examining the relationships between innovation, on the one hand, and market power and firm size, on the other. The links between innovation, market structure and firm size are usually attributed, by different authors, to the contribution of Schumpeter in his *Capitalism, Socialism and Democracy*. It has been alleged that the main engine of technological progress is the large company operating in a concentrated market. A number of specific hypotheses as to why this may be the case have been advanced, most of which were already present in Schumpeter's own work.

The most important hypotheses can be summarized as follows. Innovation increases more than proportionately with firm size because: 1) R&D projects typically involve large fixed costs, and these can only be covered if sales are sufficiently large; 2) There are scale and scope economies in the production of innovations; 3) Large diversified firms are in a better position to exploit unforeseen innovations; 4) Large firms can undertake many projects at any one time and hence spread the risks of R&D; 5) Large firms have better access to external finance. In addition, innovation is higher in concentrated industries because: 6) Firms with greater market power are better able to finance R&D from their own profits; 7) Firms with greater market power can more easily appropriate the returns from innovation and hence they have better incentives to innovate.

Counterarguments have also been suggested: 1) The existence of decreasing returns to scale in the production of innovations due to loss of managerial control and the bureaucratization of the innovative activity; 2) market power based on the absence of strong competitive pressures may lead to inertia.

Reviewing the evidence on whether there is a positive effect of market structure or firm size on innovation, several authors have concluded that empirical information is inconclusive and that, on the whole, there is little empirical support for this perspective. It would also be argued that this line of research is subject to methodological problems and that the majority of these studies do not advance our understanding of the specific mechanisms relating innovation to firm size, market power or market structure.

The evidence appears to support some, but not all, of the above hypotheses. It seems that small firms face financial constraints to a larger extent than large firms, and that the ability to raise finance matters for innovation. On the other hand, there are probably no economies of scale in the production of innovations in most industries, but this has to be balanced against the existence of indivisibilities in R&D and the fact that R&D projects may involve large fixed costs in some industries. What is common in the empirical literature on the specific hypotheses as to why market power or firm size may have a positive effect on innovative activity is the emphasis placed on mechanisms which involve a one-way direction of causation: from both market structure and firm dimension to innovative performance (figure 4.1).

Figure 4.1:
The traditional view

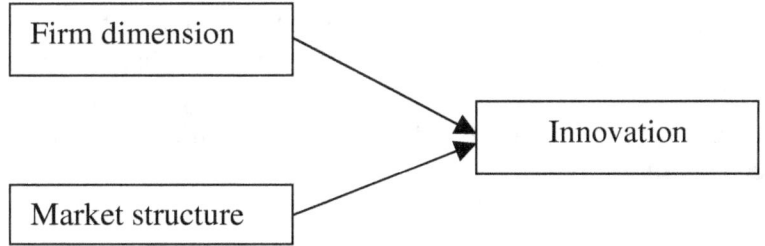

On the other hand, it is now widely accepted that the relationship between market structure, firm size and innovation is far more complex than what many studies in this area have hypothesized. Recent theoretical literature has emphasized that both innovation and market structure are endogenous variables and must be seen as simultaneously determined within a system with multiple equilibria, given all the measurable and systematic exogenous factors. Literature has also identified a number of specific mechanisms at work.

There are obviously important policy implications of the relationships between innovation and market structure, on the one hand, and innovation and firm size, on the other. As the role of innovation in promoting competitiveness and growth has become increasingly apparent, a number of policy makers have argued that antitrust laws should be relaxed, or should not be reinforced, as the short run gains from additional price competition are offset in the longer term by a slower rate of technological progress. The notion that high market concentration and large firm size are factors conducive to a faster rate of innovation has also been used in the past to justify industrial policies of support to "national champions" through public procurement and R&D subsidies. The relevance of such views depends on the validity of the hypothesis of a positive effect of market power, concentration and firm size on innovation.

However the different market structures affect economic performance and social welfare in different ways. Although a common argument in this context is that concentrated market structures may be favorable to technological progress, and hence to economic growth and higher welfare, the exercise of monopoly power is known to result in static allocative inefficiency, even if empirical estimates of the associated welfare loss vary widely. On the other hand, the static analysis of the social costs of monopoly (or oligopoly) fails to take into account the implications of alternative market structures for dynamic efficiency[22].

---

[22] As we will see in chapter 7, there may be a trade-off between short run allocative gains from increased price competition and long run welfare improvements from a higher rate of innovation under a more concentrated structure.

4.2. Appropriability, technological opportunities and cumulativeness

Contrarily to the traditional view, Malerba and Orsenigo (1995) stress the likely reverse causation and try to show that market structure depends on technology through the following characteristics of technology which are typical of each industry: appropriability; opportunity; cumulativeness; and scientific knowledge basis. They consider that higher appropriability, opportunity and cumulativeness are associated to higher concentration that occurs, for instance, in the chemical industry. Figure 4.2 shows that the reverse causation is mediated by the four factors highlighted by Malerba and Orsenigo (1995).

Figure 4.2:
The reverse causation view

In fact, the differences between the two Schumpeterian regimes are described by Malerba and Orsenigo (1995) in terms of a combination of four factors: (i) the opportunity and (ii) appropriability conditions, (iii) the cumulativeness of innovative activities and (iv) the nature of knowledge. Given such differences, industries are likely to differ with respect to their dynamic and structural properties, what would be termed "technological regimes". In this regard opportunity conditions refer to the likelihood of innovating, given a certain research effort. This may depend on, for instance, the extent to which a sector can draw from the knowledge base, the technological advances of its suppliers and customers, and major scientific advances in universities or research labs.

Appropriability conditions reflect the possibilities of protecting innovations from imitation and of appropriating the profits from an innovation. Possible appropriability devices are not only patents and secrecy, but also lead times, costs and time required for duplication, learning curve effects, superior sales efforts, and differential technical efficiency due to scale economies.

Cumulativeness conditions refer to the extent to which the innovative successes of individual firms are serially correlated. They are related to the cognitive nature of the learning process (e.g., learning by doing) and depend on the extent to which technological progress or major advances depend on the current technology stock (Nelson, 1995).

Finally, with regard to the properties of the knowledge base, Dosi, Freeman and Nelson (1988) distinguish three aspects of knowledge: (i) the level of specificity, reflecting that knowledge can be applied universally, (ii) the level of tacitness, referring to the extent to which knowledge is well articulated or whether it is more tacit, and (iii) the extent to which knowledge is publicly available, for instance in scientific and technical publications.

In the literature on technological regimes, opportunity conditions do not necessarily differ between the two Schumpeterian regimes. The differences are mainly related to differences in appropriability, cumulativeness conditions and patterns of access to knowledge. A Schumpeter Mark I regime is often characterized by low appropriability and cumulativeness conditions, and the knowledge is mainly (firm) specific, codified and simple. In a Schumpeter Mark II regime these conditions are the opposite: appropriability and cumulativeness conditions are high, while knowledge is mainly generic, tacit and complex.

Other results emerge from the recent literature respecting to certain characteristics of technology, such as the degree of continuity and certainty of technology and the extent of learning economies in innovation. Research has shown these characteristics as important determinants of the evolution of technological leadership (and of the extent of volatility in R&D-intensive industries). Another important result is that other characteristics such as the degree of product differentiation affect the extent to which high R&D intensity will be associated with a high level of market concentration. Research has also shown both technological events and random differences between firms in innovation and growth as having significant influence in shaping the evolution of market structure and innovative activity in technologically progressive industries.

4.3. Pavitt's taxonomy: techno-economic characteristics of sectors

Pavitt's taxonomy (Pavitt, 1984) was established on the basis of a descriptive analysis of the innovation process in different sectors. The empirical data consisted of a database of nearly 2000 innovations made in the UK in the period 1945 to 1979[23]. Pavitt's descriptive analysis addressed some of the major issues, which had emerged from various in depth industry studies of innovation and innovation processes. The outcome of Pavitt's analysis was a taxonomy of patterns of innovation and simultaneously a theory of innovation flows among different groups of industries grouped in four sector types. In this section, we will synthetically describe the main outcome of Pavitt's analysis: The taxonomy of sectoral patterns of innovation. Table 4.1 presents the main characteristics of sectors that are included in Pavitt's taxonomy: 'supplier-dominated', 'scale-intensive', 'science-based' and 'specialized suppliers' sectors. The sectoral taxonomy focuses on the level of industry, and provides insights to the firm size, the innovation process and the competitive parameters within the sectors.

---

[23] Pavitt (1984, p. 344).

In the 'supplier-dominated' sector, innovations are mainly process innovations, embodied in capital equipment and intermediate inputs and are originated by firms whose principal activity is outside this sector. Supplier-dominated industries include not only textiles, clothing, leather, printing and publishing and wood products, but also agricultural products. In this sector, the process of innovation is primarily a process of diffusion of best-practice capital goods and of innovative intermediate inputs, such as synthetic fibers, produced by other firms.

Table 4.1.
Pavitt's taxonomy of sectoral patterns of innovation

Sector / Variables	Supplier Dominated (SD)	Scale Intensive (SI)	Science based (SB)	Specialized suppliers (SS)
Firm size	Small firms	Large firms	Large firms	Small firms
Type of Innovation	Processes	Processes	Mixed Products and processes	Products
Locus of innovation	External	Production	R&D departments	Decentra-lized
Sources of innovation	Specialized suppliers	Production and specialized suppliers	Universities and research centers	Science based firms / customers
Means of appropriability	Tacit knowledge	Tacit knowledge and entry barriers	Patents and entry barriers	Tacit knowledge / reputation
Competitive parameter	Price	Price /quality	Performance / quality / price	Quality / perfor-mance
Industries	Textiles clothing, leather	Automobiles	Pharmaceuticals / microelectronics	Mechanical engineering
Learning	Learning by using	Learning by doing / Learning by using	Learning by searching/ Learning by doing	Learning by interacting / Learning by doing

In a 'scale-intensive' sector innovation concerns both processes and products; production activities generally involve mastering complex systems and, often, manufacturing complex products; Economies of scale of various sorts are significant; firms tend to be large, they produce a relatively high proportion of their own process technology, they devote a relatively high proportion of their own resources to innovation, and tend to vertically integrate into the manufacturing of their own equipment. This group includes transport equipment, some electric consumer durables, metal manufacturing, food products, glass and cement.

In the 'science-based' sector, innovation is directly linked to technical paradigms made possible by scientific advances; opportunity is very high; innovative activities are formalized in R&D laboratories; a high proportion of their product innovation enters a wide number of sectors as capital or intermediate inputs; firms tend to be large. This group includes the electronics industry and most of the chemical industry.

In the 'specialized suppliers' sector, innovative activities relate primarily to product innovations which enter other sectors as capital inputs. Firms tend to be relatively small; they operate in close contact with their users and embody a specialized knowledge in design and equipment building. Typically, this group includes mechanical and instrument engineering.

In subsequent versions of his taxonomy, Pavitt has added another category to classify emerging 'information-intensive' firms, which have their main source of technological accumulation in the advanced processing of data and are typical in sectors or industries such as banking, retailing, internet, software, and so on. According to this rationale, there would be a fifth sector called 'information-intensive' sector.

As described above, different sectors present a different capacity of technology accumulation. Having the majority of technology flows origin in the science based sector and, at a small scale, in the specialized suppliers sector (see figure 4.3), then it is opportune to ask some questions: Is the emergence of a dynamic technology trajectory possible which will change the dominant sector of the Pavitt's taxonomy? Will the innovation systems and policy have any role to play in such virtuous transitions? If the answer is yes, what is the role?

Figure 4.3.
Technology flows in Pavitt's taxonomy

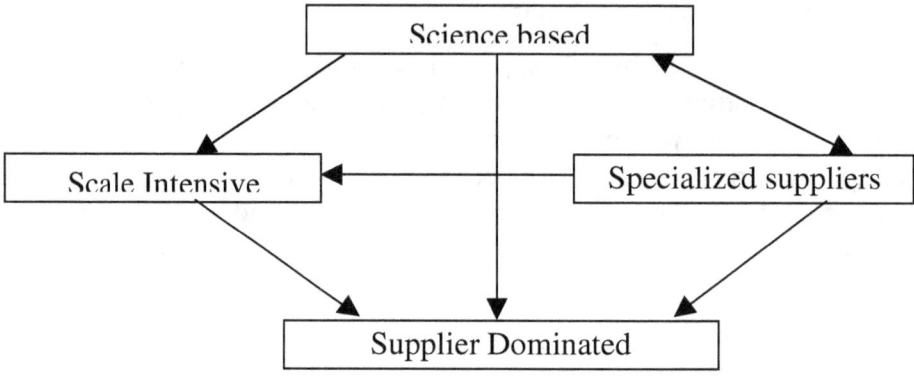

4.4. Dynamics of Pavitt's taxonomy: application to the industrialization analyses

In order to understand the dynamics of Pavitt's taxonomy it is important to consider some concepts disentangled by Pavitt. This author considers the need to distinguish between four different but related concepts. First, productive capacity is defined as a set of productive resources necessary to production (machinery and equipment goods, competencies of labor force, organizing systems, etc.), while technological capability is referred not only to productive resources, but also to resources necessary to the technological change (knowledge, experience, institutional linkages, skills, etc.). Second, while on the one hand, technical change is defined as the introduction of technology embodied in new products and/or new plants through major investment projects, technological accumulation consists of any process by which the resources for generating and managing technical change are increased or strengthened.

Pavitt showed two different patterns in the course of development: one typical of pioneer countries in industrialization, and the other visible in the new industrialized countries (NICs). While in the pioneer countries in industrialization, notably in the UK and in the US, technological development began with the main aim of solving the scarcity of resources (or reducing the use of the relatively more expensive factor). The enforcing of the technological capability was done side by side with the increase of the productive capacity. Technological change in some sectors induced technological change in other sectors. Partly, this was possible because pioneer countries controlled the general-purpose technologies, with application in several sectors.

NICs have experienced more difficulty in establishing links between the productive capacity and the technological capability, because the increase in productive capacity is based on imported equipments. The availability of specific technologies is easy when we deal with 'supplier-dominated' sectors, but in other sectors it is difficult to gather the needed technologies. Additionally, the intersectoral linkages are weak.

Has the technology policy a role to play in enhancing the technological accumulation in developing countries? Consider the different sectors of the Pavitt taxonomy, what is the role of technology policy in enforcing technological accumulation in NICs? Firstly, we must emphasize that at the beginning of the development process there was no explicit role for technological policy. The most important government policy has been the trade policy. Looking at the trade policy we can see two different patterns: while in Asia there was a relative neutrality between domestic market and external market (i.e., low nominal and effective protection) and in some cases under valuation of exchange rate to incentive exports, in Latin America the high and long-lasting protection of domestic market was notorious.

This had consequences on the imports of external developed technologies: In Asia imports of technologies embodied in machines and equipments were easier and cheaper than in Latin America. Consequently, the growth of employment and of TFP (total factor productivity) was higher in labor-intensive sectors of Asian countries than in Latin American ones.

Concerning the second question, we must note that in the first stages of development, the accumulation of technology is influenced by factor accumulation and by intersectoral linkages, but in the late stages, the level of technical knowledge can be a source of comparative advantages, reflected in the productive know-how, in the capital goods design, in the *reverse engineering* capacity, etc. Recognizing these advantages and limitations, East Asian economies have developed technological policies that have become a fundamental component of the development process. In these countries, technological accumulation was quicker than in other new industrialized countries. In technological terms, the evolution began in the supplier-dominated sector, followed by 'scale-intensive', 'specialized suppliers' sectors and continued towards the 'Science-based' sector.

*

*   *

Exercises and review questions

4.1. Evolutionary theories put the firm at the center of the technological process. Why? Justify your answer (Do not forget to mention the reasons for the central role of the firm).

4.2. Respecting the ways innovative activities take place along time, Schumpeter identified two major patterns of innovative activities. Write down a small essay on the above statement. (Do not forget to characterize the mentioned two patterns and to show how these patterns are associated to the market structure).

4.3. Malerba and Orsenigo (1995) criticize both the traditional view on the characteristics of firms and simultaneously dispute the direction of causality between market structure and technology. Make a small essay about the contribution of these two authors for explaining the patterns of innovation.

4.4. Regarding Keith Pavitt's taxonomy, characterize and compare, from the point of view of learning and technical change, the "supplier-dominated sectors" with the "specialized suppliers" sectors.

Chapter 5.

INNOVATION AND TERRITORY

Summary
Externalities, increasing returns and economic growth. Proximity and tacit knowledge. Milieu, industrial district, networks and clusters. Creative class and creative cities. Diversity, tolerance, talent and high technology.

Introduction

It is a well-known fact that modern economic growth has been accompanied by industrialization and urbanization. Industrialization often goes together with spatial agglomeration, whatever the term used to describe this grouping phenomenon: *industrial district*, *spatial agglomeration*, *industrial concentration*, *cluster*, and so on. Regions all over the world have all experienced a path of spatial clustering led by SMEs (small and medium enterprises) during the course of industrialization. Both policy-makers and development agencies generally assume that industrial agglomerations play a key role in economic development. Usually empirical studies do not contradict this thesis. So, the way firms are geographically located is assumed as a relevant factor in innovation and economic growth and authors, both in regional science and economic geography traditions, have emphasized the role played by territory in innovation and technological change.

In regional economics, the term 'territory' is used to mean the aggregate effect of the following elements: a) a system of localized externalities, both pecuniary (where their advantages are appropriated through market transactions) and technological (when advantages are exploited by simple proximity to the source); b) a system of localized production activities, traditions, skills and know-how; c) a system of localized proximity relationships which constitute a 'capital' – of a social, psychological and political nature – in that they enhance the static and dynamic productivity of local factors; d) a system of cultural elements and values which attribute sense and meaning to local practices and structures, and define local identities; these acquire an economic value whenever they can be transformed into marketable products – goods, services and assets – or they boost the internal capacity to exploit local potentials; e) a system of rules and practices defining a local governance model.

So the territory where firm is located plays a crucial role, both in static and dynamic terms, on the competitiveness of the firm. However, there are several theories that highlight, in different ways, the importance of the local environment for economic transformation and growth. Some of these can be catalogued as belonging to "regional the cluster theory", but a number of basic concepts are common to most of other different theoretical perspectives, which have a past well before cluster's fashion. In order to systematize some such perspectives, in the remainder of this chapter we'll begin by dealing with the role of infrastructure and externalities. Section 2 takes in hand the role of proximity and tacit knowledge on the innovation processes and analyses the concepts of innovative milieu and industrial district. The concepts of social capital, clusters and networks are treated in section 3. Finally, the analysis of Richard Florida's view about creative cities together with a reflection about the relationship between diversity, talent and technology conclude the chapter.

5.1. Territory, infrastructure and externalities

a) Urban hierarchy and infrastructure

Are there territorial determinants of the innovation and diffusion processes? If yes, are the territorial determinants fairly distributed throughout the national territory?

In order to answer the first question, we can define territorial determinants as a set of spatial factors external to firms which are associated to technological progress (giving rise to external economies), such as: a) the agglomeration economies associated to the Urban Hierarchy; b) the Collective and Technological Infrastructure. Respecting to the urban hierarchy, we know that the city is a location of concentration of qualified and specialized human resources, essential to the processes of innovation and absorption of innovation and that it is also characterized by agglomeration of services of various kinds (trade, education [universities], and also specialized services to support innovation).

Respecting to infrastructure, collective infrastructure is important to the well-being of the general population and is a factor of attraction of high skilled human resources. Technological infrastructure has significant importance to firms as well, because they can externalize some functions if the infrastructure is located nearby. There are several types of technological infrastructure, as for instance, the Technological Center, which provides technical services (for instance, quality control), technical formation and applied research, the Science & Technology Park and also some entrepreneurial associations which have an important role to play in providing services to their members, such as professional formation support to develop some innovative projects, etc.

b) Agglomeration externalities

The *agglomeration* externalities constitute the basis of a long lasting theoretical perspective on the effects of industrial concentration, ever since Alfred Marshall in his book *Principles of Economics* described how companies get advantages as a result of being located in close geographic proximity to each other's businesses. Potter and Watts (2011) have grouped these advantages in a "trinity of agglomeration economies" (local pool of skilled labor, local supplier linkages, and local knowledge spillovers), from which firms should receive increasing returns.

Commonly speaking, agglomeration externalities are advantages got by companies from being located in regional environments where there are many other businesses. The financial industry in the City of London, the textile and footwear manufacturing in northern Italy, the ICT industries in Silicon Valley and the Hollywood film industry are only a few of the best known examples highlighted in the literature of industrial agglomerations characterized by high externalities. Benefits derived by firms in a particular industry from locating close to each other are termed *localization economies*, while the gains obtained by firms from many industries by locating in the same area or city would be termed *urbanization economies*.

David and Rosenbloom (1990) ask why people and firms tend to congregate spatially. The fundamental reason is that individual companies benefit from the high spatial concentration of businesses although agglomeration can also cause negative effects. The external effects may arise both because of pecuniary externalities and knowledge spillovers (see Krugman, 1991). David and Rosenbloom (1990, p. 349) explore, in a stylized approach, agglomeration pecuniary externalities "that tend to reduce the prices at which primary inputs can be purchased as more and more of those inputs come to be assembled at the locale in question". Of course, although externalities are created through co-location, each individual company can only influence the conditions to a very small degree.

118

As mentioned above, agglomeration externalities are usually listed in two types: localization externalities and urbanization externalities. However, more recently two other types appeared in the literature: Jacob's externalities, which refer to economies external to the firm coming from the local variety of industries (Jacobs, 1969), and related variety benefits (Frenken *et al.*, 2007).

There are many different types of localization externalities, and their nature also depends on which other companies share the regional environment (businesses of the same industry, or companies working in other, but still related, sectors), but the best known in literature are the following: a) better access to the market for goods and to suppliers, labor pooling, and easy flow of technology know-how (Marshall, 1920); b) transforming into many small investments a large lump-sum investment (Schmitz, 1995) and so lowering capital entry barriers (Ruan and Zhang, 2009); c) speeding the flow of ideas (Glaeser and Gottlieb, 2009) and increasing innovation, which results from technology linkages among related industries (Scherer 1982; Feldman and Audretsch 1999).

The agglomeration externalities can be named static if they affect the TFP (total factor productivity) of firms through only an increase in the efficiency of the technologies already in use. This increase in efficiency usually comes from a reduction of costs caused by concentration, such as reduced transportation and transaction costs for intra-organizational exchange and access to external markets. But the external economies can influence the development and the relative well being of different regions in the long run by affecting TFP in another way: by increasing the innovative capacity of firms. That is, they can act dynamically. When this happens, the literature usually names them as dynamic externalities. So, from a policy perspective, it is important to distinguish between static and dynamic externalities although both types can increase productivity.

5.2. The role of proximity on the innovation processes: innovative milieu and industrial district

a) Proximity

The benefits of proximity have been highlighted by numerous authors following several traditions: Proximity makes greater access to tacit knowledge possible, opens opportunities for cooperation and collaboration and gives the neighborhood firms power to influence customers, markets, or policies. Proximity also gives higher access to experienced labor and allows firms to be more familiarized with competitors' products and processes and to check their own innovation and targets. In spite of the influence of recent innovations, as the Internet and overnight delivery, proximity keeps being helpful for mapping the growth of territorial innovation systems and even crucial for some production inputs, such as key equipment and components that are knowledge-intensive and/or result from interactive research and design.

The importance of proximity in the transfer of tacit knowledge does not depend solely on geographical distance, as traditional explanations of the time and cost advantages of co-location tend to conclude. Although geographic co-location increases the probability of interaction to occur, proximity also has a *relational* dimension (Boschma, 2005). It is important to keep this in mind, since the exchange of strategically important information and knowledge requires mutual trust between the parties. In this sense, proximity is very related with the social capital concept highlighted by Putnam (1993), as we will see in the next section.

So, proximity, which is the key characteristic of a region, possesses not only a spatial (geographical) dimension, but also a *relational* dimension. This involves aspects such as trust and understanding (Boschma, 2005). Although much of the literature agrees that spatial proximity often generates, or at least encourages, the emergence of relational proximity, this is not an automatic result from geographic proximity, because trust between individuals and firms is basically an effect of how long a particular relationship lasts, how frequent communication is, and whether they engage in repeated collaborations. So, despite how close two actors are in terms of geographical distance, a lack of trust between them can lead to the failure of wished interaction and knowledge exchange.

In the case of the tacit dimension of knowledge, labor mobility is probably one of the most common channels for knowledge transfer between organizations in a region. Labor mobility also has a clear territorial dimension, as the mobility of individuals between regions, and even more so between countries, is very limited. This is why the experience of human resources has remained a primary reason of agglomeration, since successful firms depend on a continuous flow of workers, skilled with the necessary ability and with the knowledge of the business which are needed to both routine and unforeseen situations.

b) Milieu and Innovation

The local 'milieu' may be defined as a set of territorial relationships encompassing a production system, different economic and social actors, a specific culture and a representation system in a coherent way, and generating a dynamic collective learning process. This specific culture includes not only the system of rules and particular values of a locality (village, town, region, etc.), but also the so-called relational capital, which corresponds to the knowledge resulting from the act of working together (Camagni, 1991).

The milieu of firms has important roles to play in the innovation process both in terms of static efficiency (TFP increases in the technologies already in use) and in dynamic efficiency (innovative capacity of firms), because it allows a reduction of the uncertainty that characterizes the processes of innovation and imitation. Relating to information, the milieu has a double role in helping to decrease uncertainty (Camagni, 1991). On the one hand, it helps circulation and decoding of information and on the other it helps the development of collective learning processes.

In their economic behavior and decision-making processes firms face three important kinds of static uncertainty: a) static uncertainty, coming from an *information gap*' linked to the complexity, the width and the cost of the information collection activity; in the real world, the firm is usually left with a huge lack of relevant information about the occurrence of already known events; b) static uncertainty, coming from an *assessment gap*' linked to the difficulty of inspecting; ex-ante the qualitative, mainly hidden, characteristics of inputs, components, production factors, and technical equipment; c) static uncertainty, coming from a *competence gap*', linked to the firm's limited ability of processing and understanding available information; the existence of technical problems whose solutions are obscure is an example of this wide category of situations.

But firms also face two important kinds of dynamic uncertainty: d) dynamic uncertainty coming from the so called *'C-D gap'* (competence-decision gap); uncertainty in this case involves the impossibility of precisely assessing the outcomes of alternative actions, even in presence of full and free information on past events — due to the complexity of the decision problems themselves and inherently imperfect foresight; e) dynamic uncertainty coming from a 'control gap': the outcomes of present actions depend in fact on the dynamic interaction among independent decisions of many actors about which the firm has a minimum control (Camagni, 1991).

c) Industrial District

One type of territorial/industrial organization in which a large importance is attributed to the milieu is called ID (Industrial District). This can be defined as a set of SMEs (Small and Medium Enterprises) agglomerated in a specific space and linked by a strong division of labor. The concept of ID has its roots in the "industrial atmosphere" of Marshall (1890) and was lately developed by Becattini (1979) and Garofoli (1992), amongst others. The agglomeration of firms helps the reduction of transport and transaction costs, which is the result of geographical, cultural and social proximity between partners.

This type of territorial organization is very frequent in South European countries. For instance, in Italy the industrial *districts* of Prato (textiles) and Sassuolo (ceramics); in France, Besançon and Morteau (clocks), Choletais (footwear); in Spain, (the region of Valles); in Portugal, Vale do Ave (textiles), Entre Douro e Vouga (footwear), Marinha Grande (glass). But it is also possible to find examples in countries such as Germany (Baden-Württemberg), Denmark (Jutland), Sweden (Småland) and even Silicon Valley in the USA.

The existent Industrial Districts share some common characteristics. First of all, they are characterized by the existence of a strong competitive environment populated by small firms without a leader firm. The SMEs are strongly specialized around a sector or a productive branch of activity and are generally open to foreign trade. The ID is also characterized by an endogenous entrepreneurship: the new entrepreneurs and the owners of new firms are usually previous workers in firms of the same ID.

Industrial Districts are also characterized by vertical and territorial integration. In fact, firms are strongly integrated in the territory, as is apparent by the high density of linkages with the local milieu. This integration allows firms to benefit from external agglomeration economies, which may not only be urbanization economies – external to firm and to industry – but also localization economies – external to firm but internal to industry. But IDs are also characterized by vertical integration between firms which permits a high capacity of externalizing functions and allows each firm to easily attain the optimum scale.

Respecting Static and Dynamic Efficiency issues, the Industrial District usually presents a good performance in terms of static efficiency (i.e., improvements in the technologies already in use) and also a good performance in terms of dynamic efficiency in what respects to incremental innovation in the dominant activities in the district. But there are few examples of inter-sectoral transference of resources. This low mobility of resources delays the structural change and can be a cause of failure of ID when the external environment changes, for instance, when a new foreign competitor appears with lower production costs in the dominant activity of the ID.

5.3. Social capital, networks and clusters

a) Social capital

Social capital can be defined as the application or use of social norms of reciprocity, trust and exchange for political or economic purposes. The principle behind the notion of social capital is rather simple and straightforward: people invest in social relations with the aim of obtaining the expected returns. That is, individuals engage in interactions and networking in order to make profits or any other benefit. Generally, four explanations can be offered as to why embedded resources in social networks will enhance the outcomes of actions.

First, social capital facilitates the flow of information. In the usual imperfect market situations, individuals placed in certain strategic locations and/or hierarchical positions are better informed on market needs and demands and thus social ties can provide an individual with useful information about opportunities and choices otherwise not available. Similarly, these ties may indicate to an organization, either in the production or consumption market, and to its agents the availability and interest of an otherwise unrecognized individual. Such information would reduce the transaction cost for the organization to recruit "better" skilled, in technical or cultural knowledge, individuals and for individuals to find "better" organizations, which can use their capital and provide appropriate rewards.

Second, these social ties may exert influence on the agents who play a critical role in decisions involving individuals and firms. Due to their strategic locations and positions (e .g., authority or supervisory capacities), some social ties also carry more valued resources and apply greater power in organizational agents' decision making.

Third, social ties, and their acknowledged relationships to the individual, may be considered by the organization or its agents as certifications of the individual's social credentials, some of which reflect the individual's accessibility to resources through social networks and relations – his/her social capital. "Standing behind" the individual by these ties reassures the organization (and its agents) that the individual can provide "added" resources beyond the individual's personal capital, some of which may be useful to the organization.

Finally, social relations are expected to reinforce identity and recognition. Being assured and recognized of one's merit as an individual and a member of a social group sharing similar interests and resources not only provides emotional support but also public acknowledgment of one's claim to certain resources. These reinforcements are essential for the maintenance of mental health and the entitlement to resources. These four elements – information, influence, social credentials and reinforcement – may explain why social capital works in instrumental and expressive actions not accounted for by forms of personal capital such as financial capital or human capital.

b) Networks and clusters

Both networks and clusters are agglomerations of firms with certain common interests. According to Porter (1998, p. 78) "clusters are geographic concentrations of interconnected companies and institutions in a particular field". But, contrasting with networks, neither "membership" in an organization nor cooperation is required to be "in" a cluster. Free riders, just by virtue of location, are able to benefit from non-exclusive external economies that spill over people and organizations localized under the cluster influence. This constitutes an important difference between clusters and other forms of association.

According to Rosenfeld (2005), clusters are informal and inclusive while the other forms of association (as for instance, professional or industrial associations and networks) are formal and exclusive, with members gaining advantages over non-members. In clusters, free riders are not only unavoidable but also, and perhaps more importantly, contribute to making clusters more powerful. In every cluster not only a sufficient provision of technicians, and sales staff, but also a labor force experienced on the specific milieu in which the cluster functions are crucial.

Economic history shows that the origins of clusters are diverse and wide-ranging: we find clusters that result from one or two successful companies with employees with an entrepreneurial vision; or from the expansion of value added chains around very large firms; or even from efforts by laid off employees to use their competences in innovative ways. But, although their origin may be varied, spontaneity, *relational* dimension of proximity, tacit knowledge, interdependence and some informality in belonging are key characteristics of all of the best-known (e.g., Californian wine cluster, fashion cluster in Paris).

To sum up, according to the social capital perspective, social capital, understood as trust, common rules, connections and networks etc., which are present in clusters, is of crucial importance for creating learning environments and, consequently, for transforming knowledge into product or process innovations.

5.4. Florida's thesis and creative cities

According to the literature about proximity and social capital, which inspires the potential advantages of industrial districts, networks and clusters, innovation within industries will have better chances when strong ties between people are present. However, Richard Florida (2002a) comes to a different conclusion when he analyses the creative class. He argues that social capital as defined by Putnam (1993) is exclusive in the sense that social interaction is based on communities of likeness.

According to Florida, the social capital approach faces a problem: its exclusive nature eliminates diversity and hence strangles space for innovative thought. Simultaneously, the exclusive nature of strong ties makes it very difficult for outsiders, e.g. migrants, to enter social circles. Florida links idea-generation and thus innovativeness to the availability of heterogeneity of voices and perspectives. So, in his view, weak ties allow a much faster inclusion into communities favoring rapid absorption of new ideas as well as adjustment of norms and values.

The Florida thesis sees the creative class as a catalyst of change and innovation. Additionally, the more heterogeneous the creative class is, the more possibilities it opens for combining and mixing different ideas and viewpoints which in turn leads to a large supply of possible innovations. Furthermore, this fact, together with other factors such as labor markets characterized by high demand for qualified personnel, cultural diversity and tolerance, low entry barriers and high levels of urban service, largely determines the economic geography of talent and of creativity, both of which display concentration in large cities.

Analyzing US economy, Florida considers that the tremendous influx of talented immigrants has been of critical importance to American success in the last century. The real advantage of the United States lies in its ability to attract these economic drivers (creative people, innovative ideas) from around the world. Additionally, he considers that today's global economy centers on competition for people rather than for goods and services. Students are a leading indicator of global talent flows. The countries and regions that attract them have a leg up on retaining them and also on attracting other pools of foreign talent-scientists, researchers, inventors, and entrepreneurs.

According to Florida, the creative class has a core formed by scientists, engineers, architects, designers, educators, artists, musicians, and entertainers, and all other similar professions whose economic function is to create new ideas, new technology, or new content. Florida also included other activities such as creative professions of business and finance, law, health care, and related fields, in which knowledge workers engage in complex problem solving that involves a great deal of independent judgment.

In order to explain the creativity-competitiveness connection, Florida suggests that the heterogeneity found in cosmopolitan cities is the backbone of creativity and thus of innovations. He argues that companies agglomerate in cities to draw on the concentration of talented people who generate innovation and economic growth. In fact, he considers that competition for talent occurs not only between nations but also between cities and regions just as competition in many industries occurs at the business-unit, rather than the company, level. New York, for instance, competes with London and Hong Kong; San Francisco rivals Dublin, Vancouver, Stockholm, and Sydney. While comprehensive regional data do not exist, several studies do give a detailed picture of areas inside Canada and Australia.

According to data amassed by Stolarick, Gertler, Gates, and Vinodrai, and cited by Florida (2004), the percentage of workers in the creative classes in Toronto (36.4%), Montreal (35.0%), and Vancouver (35.2%) rival those in the leading American regions. Of America's ten most populous regions, only the Washington, DC (39.8%), and Boston (36.5%) areas do better. Toronto and Vancouver have the highest concentration of immigrants in North America, with 43.7% and 37.5% of their respective populations hailing from other countries. By comparison only 24.4% of New Yorkers were born outside the United States and only 30.9% of Los Angelinos. Of course, percentages do not give the full picture. The sheer number of creative class members found in a metropolis like New York is far greater than in, say, Toronto. But the percentages do shed light on which cities are fostering creative cultures and will, therefore, be attractive to more creative types in the future.

Australia's leading regions are also well positioned to compete as global creative centers, according to detailed benchmarking data compiled by the National Institute of Economic and Industry Research, and cited by Florida (2004). Its two largest regions, Sydney and Melbourne, would rank approximately fourth or fifth if they were U.S. regions. Their creative classes are similar in size to those of Boston or Seattle. The Australian study compiled data for particular inner-city neighborhoods, as well. Creative occupations make up fully half the workforce in both central Sydney (51.1%) and central Melbourne (49.5%) — far greater than in virtually any inner city in the U.S. Both these centers have high percentages of immigrants (42.5% and 35.6% respectively) and are breeding grounds of fine art, fashion, music, and street culture.

5.4.1. Diversity, talent and technology

To confirm his ideas, Florida uses a simple model known as the three Ts (tolerance, talent and technology), as is depicted in figure 5.1[24].

Figure 5.1.
Relationship between diversity, talent and high technology

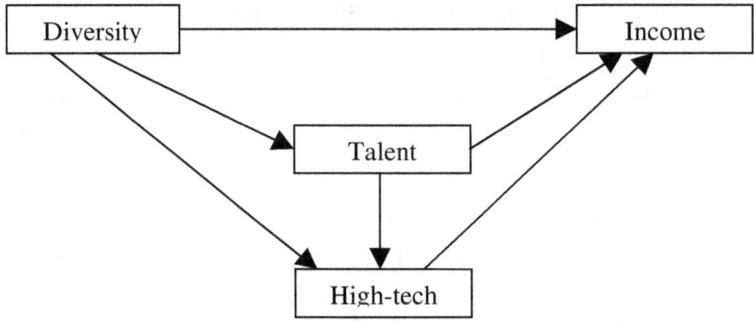

Source: adapted from Florida (2002a)

In this model, diversity is propelled by tolerance. Tolerance refers to the acceptance of individual differences and an absence of pressure towards conformity. Tolerance also underpins the ability to attract talents, as the creative class tends to gravitate towards urban areas characterized by bohemian values and openness. According to Florida, cities with the highest degree of ethnic, social and sexual tolerance are capable of attracting the most promising talents on a global scale. The logic in the argument is simply that it allows for a global sourcing for

---

[24] In the figure, diversity appears as a proxy of tolerance, because Florida considers that diversity is propelled by tolerance.

the best ideas; hence, a city located in a non-tolerant environment will push valuable innovative inputs away.

As is apparent from figure 5.1, talents and tolerance only constitute two out of the three pillars underpinning the successful development of innovative industries and regions; a technological foundation is also required. The outcome of attracting and retaining a pool of talents should be directed towards high-tech industries as they are considered to be the most important means of generating regional growth. "Each is a necessary but by itself insufficient condition: To attract creative people, generate innovation and stimulate economic growth, a place must have all three" (talents, tolerance and high-tech industries).

Through quantitative studies, Florida (2002a) and his colleagues found correlation between ethnical, social and sexual diversity, concentration of talent and clustering of high-tech industries. Based on empirical investigations, Florida and Gates (2002) conclude that '...a city's diversity – its level of tolerance for a wide level of people – is the key to its success in attracting talented people.

5.4.2. Conclusion

In sum, the role of creative cities in promoting regional economic development has called for new competitive policy measures. Today, cities and regions compete on at least two fronts: Firstly, cities try to attract investments by forming an inspiring business climate. This is done by providing attractive space for location, by actively guiding firms through public administration and bureaucracy, etc. Secondly, and narrowly linked, the ability to attract and retain highly skilled labor is crucial to the current and future prosperity of cities.

So, according to Florida's results, to attract firms is not enough; the 'right' people also need to be attracted. Thus economic growth calls for complementing policies for attracting firms (business climate) with policies for attracting people (people's climate). People's climate can be understood as a series of ingredients that spice up the city making it 'cool'. On the supply side, this covers different amenities such as cultural organization, bars, nightclubs, parks, etc. A well functioning welfare state providing social, educational and economic comfort and security is important, too.

Exercises and review questions

5.1. Some authors, following the seminal work of Roberto Camagni, argue that the milieu of firms has an important role in the innovation process. Write a small essay about this topic. (Do not forget to define milieu and to indicate the role played by the milieu both in terms of static and dynamic efficiency.

5.2. While some authors emphasize the importance of proximity in enhancing innovation, others stress the role played by social capital. However, there is no significant difference between the two approaches. Do you agree? Justify your answer.

5.3. The concept of ID (Industrial District) has its roots in the "industrial atmosphere" of Marshall (1890) and was lately developed by Becattini (1979) and Garofoli (1992), among others. Define and characterize the ID prevalent in South European countries.

Chapter 6
INNOVATION SYSTEMS

Summary
Innovation System: concept and functions; National Innovation System (NIS); Regional Innovation System (RIS). RIS and knowledge base. RIS taxonomy: The Asheim and Gertler analysis.

In a chapter dedicated to IS (innovation systems) it is opportune to begin with a definition of IS. The Innovation System's approach is recent: It has begun with the seminal works of Freeman (1987), Lundvall (1992) and Nelson (1993). But in spite of being recent, the IS approach has become very established in a very short period of time. It is widely used in academic contexts and also as a framework for innovation policy-making.

6.1. Innovation System: concept and functions

Edquist (1997, p.14) reviewed the IS literature and defined a system of innovation as "all important economic, social, political, organizational, and other factors that influence the development, diffusion, and use of innovations." This means that the IS approach is about the determinants of innovations, not about their consequences. It is important to understand what a system is. In general a system consists of two kinds of entities: There are firstly, some kinds of *components* and secondly, there are *relations* between these. There should be reasons why a certain array of components and relations has been chosen to constitute the system; they form a *whole*. It must be possible to discriminate the system in relation to the rest of the world; i.e., it must be possible to identify the *boundaries* of the system. However, only in exceptional cases is the system closed in the sense that it has nothing to do with the rest of the world[25].

Edquist (1997) characterized IS in several dimensions. Maybe the most important one was that innovations are normally seen as based on learning that is interactive between organizations; firms do not generally innovate in isolation. Another important feature is that institutions are considered to be crucial elements in all versions of the IS approach (Edquist 1997). In addition, all versions of the IS approach consider innovation processes to be evolutionary (Edquist 1997). These characteristics of the IS approach are seen as major advances in the study and understanding of innovation processes.

The main components of IS are organizations and institutions. It is important to distinguish between these two types of components. Organizations are formal structures with an explicit purpose and they are consciously created (Edquist and Johnson 1997). They are players or actors. Some important organizations in IS are companies (which can be suppliers, customers or competitors in relation to other companies), universities, venture capital organizations and public innovation policy agencies. On the other hand, institutions are sets of common habits, routines, established practices, rules, or laws that regulate the relations and interactions between individuals, groups and organizations (Edquist and Johnson 1997). They are the rules of the game. Examples of important institutions in IS are patent laws and norms influencing the relations between universities and firms.

---

[25] That part of the rest of the world that in some sense is important for the system is called its *environment*.

The *relations between organizations and institutions* are important for innovations and for the operation of systems of innovation. An important characteristic of the IS approach is the mutual embeddedness, that is, organizations are strongly influenced and shaped by institutions; organizations can be said to be 'embedded' in an institutional environment or set of rules which include the legal system, norms, standards, etc. But institutions are also 'embedded' in organizations. Examples are firm specific practices with regard to bookkeeping or concerning the relations between managers and employees, which a lot of institutions develop inside firms. Hence, there is a complicated two-way relationship of mutual embeddedness between institutions and organizations, and this relationship influences innovation processes and thereby also both the performance and change of systems of innovation. (Edquist and Johnson, 1997). The institutions shape (and are shaped by) the actions of the organizations and the relations between them.

Figure 6.1 represents an IS where some interactions are visible linking the different components of the system with the firm in a central place. The figure shows the mutual embeddedness between institutions and organizations. For instance, the efforts played by firms in order to improve their performance will be larger or shorter in line with the available incentives. But such efforts can be spent either in equipment or in licenses of technology, according to the norms and routines that characterize the technology imports. Additionally, the access of firms to the knowledge produced in Universities and other organizations of S&T (science and technology) depends on interaction practices between firms and producers of codified knowledge, which in turn depends on the use of such knowledge by firms. This is the reason why there is a double arrow linking each pair of the IS components.

Figure 6.1.
IS: interactions between components

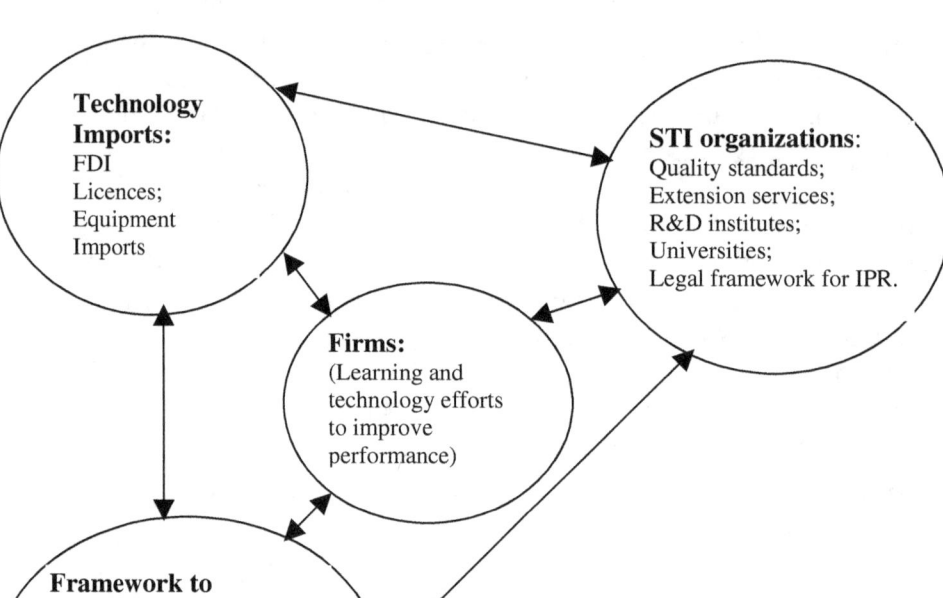

The figure necessarily gives a very simplified picture of an IS. The system depends on other factors, as for instance the concept of innovation[26]. When the innovation concept has been specified, it becomes crucial to identify all the important factors influencing the

---

[26] The concept of innovation influences the elements included in the system. For instance, if we consider only technological innovations we will have a system with some different elements from another system that considers innovation as a broader phenomenon.

development, diffusion and use of these innovations. So, it is not sufficient to identify the main components of IS and the relations between them. We must also explicitly address what 'happens' in the system. What do the organizations do in relation to innovation processes? How do institutions constrain/prevent or stimulate the organizations to do certain things related to innovation processes? What role does the relations between the components in the systems play for innovation processes? What is the overall function of the system as a whole – constituted by the components and the relations between them?

Systems of innovation may be supranational, national or sub national (regional, local). Whether a system of innovation should be spatially or sectorally delimited – or both - depends on the object of study. All the approaches mentioned above may be fruitful – but for different purposes or objects of study. Generally, the approaches complement each other rather than exclude each other. This is because it is a limitation to talk about globalization and regionalization without addressing the national level. Therefore, it is useful to consider sectoral and regional systems of innovation as parts of national ones.

6.2. National Innovation System

National Innovation Systems can be quite different from each other, e.g., with regard to specialization of production, resources spent on R&D, etc. For example, industrial production in the United States is much more specialized in the production of R&D intensive ('hi-tech') products than is industrial production in the EU (Fagerberg 2001, Edquist and Texier 1996). Further, within the EU, R&D intensities vary greatly between countries. In addition, organizations and institutions constituting components of the systems may be different. For example, research institutes and company-based research departments may be important organizations in one country (e.g. Japan) while research universities may perform a similar function in another (e.g. the United States). Institutions such as laws, norms, and values also differ considerably between systems.

The NIS approach has some policy implications: first, innovation policy is public action that influences technical change and other kinds of innovations. It includes elements of research and development (R&D) policy, technology policy, infrastructure policy, regional policy and education policy. This means that innovation policy goes beyond science and technology (S&T) policy, which mainly focuses on stimulating basic science as a public good from the supply side. Innovation policy also includes public action influencing innovations from the demand side.

6.3. Regional Innovation System (RIS)

At the same time as in NIS the *boundaries* of the system coincide with the national frontiers the RIS corresponds to the territory within the region. However, in the literature there are two not coincident ways of defining a region. While the traditional view considers a region as an area characterized by economic specificity, administrative homogeneity, and shared culture, the RIS perspective defines region as a system of collective order maintained through trust and reliability. This definition allows to consider the RIS as characterized by economic coordination and emphasizing the importance of cultural factors, including trust, cooperation, and social network relationships.

In recent years the RIS evolved into a widely used analytical framework where the empirical foundation to the innovation policymaking is rooted. There are two reasons. First, innovation occurs in an institutional and social context and region is the place of economic interaction and innovation (Storper, 1997). Second, innovation can be thought of as embedded in social relationships and the regional context establishes the set of regulations, conventions and norms that stipulate behavioral roles and form expectations.

6.3.1. RIS and knowledge base

Research in regional growth has been characterized by two trends in recent years. On the one hand, the creative class approach has argued that competition for talents has increased as innovation becomes crucial for maintaining competitiveness. This has forced local and regional authorities to implement new political actions toward supplementing the traditional business orientated policies with policies orientated towards attracting and retaining people. On the other hand, the second trend argues that regional analysis and policy-making need to be disaggregated to meet the diverse needs of different regions and, due to the particularities characterizing innovative industries, drawing on different knowledge bases.

Asheim and Gertler (2005) and Asheim and Vang (2004, 2005) have criticized the highly aggregated level that characterizes Florida's work. They have argued that regional analysis and policy-making need to differentiate between the particularities characterizing innovative industries, moving beyond the aggregation, and drawing on different knowledge bases. Asheim and associates point out that while the knowledge base approach has the organization of the innovative production and the related support structure as the prime focus, the creative class approach only pays attention to retain and attract talents for broadly defined innovative activities.

But, what is a knowledge base? A knowledge base refers to several elements. First of all, it refers to a mix of tacit and codified knowledge used in a particular industry; secondly, to codification possibilities and limits; and, thirdly, to competencies and skills and the characteristics of the institutional support system (Asheim and Vang 2005).

Respecting the mix of tacit and codified knowledge — the first element in a knowledge base — it is important to make the distinction between tacit and codified knowledge. When knowledge is tacit, it is stickier and does not flow as easily across borders within organizations or in space. Knowledge stays tacit if it is complex or changeable in quality, if e.g. understanding social relationship is crucial, skilful physical behavior is needed or several different human senses are needed at the same time. This distinction is particularly important for innovation policy, given that there would be little incentives for firms, regions and nations to invest in R&D, if all knowledge were easily transformed into information that everyone could access.

The second and third elements of the knowledge base as a whole determine the needs of firms for institutional support. The individual knowledge bases of a particular industry are constituted by different mixes of tacit and codified knowledge and a different need for institutional support deriving from the nature of output. The literature differentiates between three knowledge bases: analytic, synthetic and symbolic.

The analytical knowledge base refers to industrial settings, where scientific knowledge is highly important, and where knowledge creation is often based on cognitive and rational processes. Industries drawing on an analytical knowledge base are much more dependent upon abstract formal codified knowledge than on tacit knowledge. This means that: a) knowledge inputs are often based on reviews of existing studies; b) knowledge generation is based on the application of widely shared and understood scientific principles and methods; c) knowledge processes are more formally organized (*e.g.* in R&D departments); d) outcomes of knowledge processes tend to be documented in reports, electronic files or patent descriptions.

Types of industries that rely on an analytical knowledge base correspond to the science-based sector of Pavitt's taxonomy, as for instance, genetics, biotechnology and information technology. So, industries drawing on the analytical knowledge base tend to locate and cluster around leading universities.

On the other hand, industries drawing on the synthetic knowledge base are typically located at industrial settings where the innovation mainly comes from new combinations of partly tacit and partly codified but already existing knowledge. Frequently innovation is of an incremental product type and is often developed in a user-producer interaction context aiming at solving the user's specific problems. Knowledge tends to be created inductively rather than deductively, through a process of testing, experimentation, and simulation. So, while the knowledge embodied in technical solutions is at least partially codified, tacit knowledge tends to be more important, since shop floor or office experience, on-the-job training, and learning by doing, using and interacting are crucial to knowledge generation. The synthetic knowledge base is present in e.g. plant engineering and specialized advanced industrial machinery. The industries using the synthetic knowledge base are seen in clusters and industrial districts, which imply that these industries gain from geographical proximity rather than multiculturalism and urban dynamics.

Finally, activities drawing on a symbolic knowledge base tend to be the so-called creative industries (sometimes referred to as infotainment or cultural industries), that is, film, theatre, publishing, advertising, etc. As for the synthetic knowledge base, these industries refer to industrial settings where innovation takes place mainly through the application of existing knowledge or through new combinations of knowledge, and, occasionally, through setting new technical, aesthetical or narrative standards. But, and moreover, the innovations are different from other types of knowledge bases as the products tend to be evaporative (while they might exist physically in some form, they only get the consumers' attention for a limited time span). A symbolic knowledge base tends to rely more on learning-by-doing, in the job and on training innate capabilities rather than on formal learning processes.

So, considering the knowledge base approach, the RIS can be imagined as the institutional infrastructure supporting innovation within the production structure of a region, as depicted in figure 6.2. This figure clarifies the importance of knowledge interaction processes in a RIS. While the application and exploitation of knowledge is done in firms, the generation and diffusion of knowledge has an important participation of public organizations. 'Learning by doing,' 'learning by using' and 'learning by interaction' are three complementary approaches to instilling a learning culture in industry -- that is, a culture characterized by institutional, cooperative learning that leads to innovative progress. Policy should serve as the infrastructure reinforcing this learning economy by supporting linkages between society and economy.

Figure 6.2.
RIS and knowledge generation and application

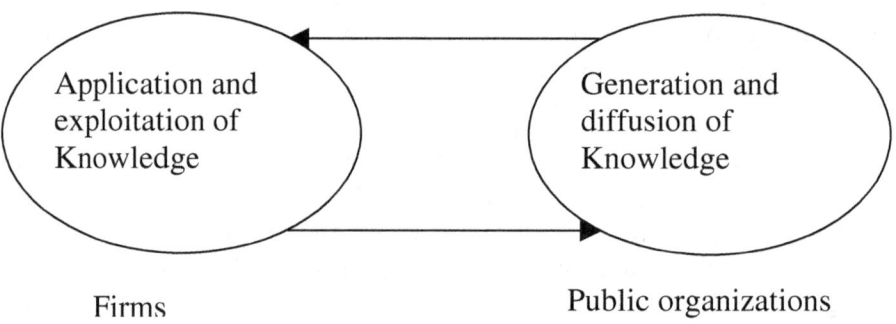

Of course, the demand for knowledge by firms depends on the type of industries, which in turn are not equally distributed by national territory. This is also a reason to consider different types of RIS.

142

6.3.2. RIS taxonomy: The Asheim and Gertler analysis

Several authors have tried to classify the different types of RIS, but one of the best-known taxonomies is due to Asheim and Gertler (2005). According to these authors there are three types of RIS: territorially embedded regional innovation system, also recognized as "grassroots RIS"; regionally networked innovation system, also called "network RIS"; and regionalized national innovation system, also known as "dirigiste RIS".

The territorially embedded regional innovation system corresponds to a system where firms (mainly those employing synthetic knowledge) base their innovation activity on localized learning processes stimulated by proximity without much direct interaction with knowledge organizations. This is the case of many South European Industrial Districts, as for instance the Italian ones.

On the other hand, a regionally networked innovation system is a regional cluster of firms surrounded by a regional supporting institutional infrastructure. It is usually the result of policy intervention to increase innovation capacity and collaboration in cooperation with local universities and R&D institutes. The basic idea is that technology transfer agencies and service centers supplement firms' competence. It is most typical of Germany, Austria, and the Nordic countries. In this RIS the policy intervention is used not only to increase collective innovation capacity but it may also be useful in counteracting technological "lock-in" within regional clusters of firms.

Finally, the regionalized national innovation system is the result of a process of clustering R&D laboratories of large firms and governmental research institutes in planned "science parks". It is a model where exogenous actors and relationships play a larger role. That is, innovation activity takes place primarily with actors outside the region (lack of local and regional embeddeness) and significant parts of the industry are more integrated into national or international innovation systems. The most notorious examples are the technopoles of France or the science parks in Japan and Taiwan.

Exercises and review questions

6.1. Innovation Systems may be supranational, national or sub national (regional, local). Define Innovation System and describe the elements that an IS includes.

6.2. "Research in regional growth has been characterised by two trends in recent years. The first is that creativity and talents are seen as parameters for regional growth. The creative class approach has argued that competition for talents has increased as innovation becomes crucial for maintaining competitiveness. (...) The second trend argues that regional analysis and policy-making need to be disaggregated to meet the diverse needs of different regions and due to the particularities characterizing innovative industries drawing on different knowledge bases."
(Høgni Kalsø Hansen, Jan Vang and Bjørn T. Asheim)

Write down a small essay upon the above statement. (Do not forget to characterize the mentioned two trends and, particularly, the different knowledge bases that the authors are considering).

6.3. Considering the Asheim and Gertler taxonomy of Regional Innovation Systems, make the distinction between the territorially embedded regional innovation system and the regionalized national innovation system.

Chapter 7

INNOVATION POLICY

Summary
Foundations of innovation policy; The "appropriability problem". Social rate and private rate of return of innovative activities. The intellectual property problematic and the use of patents. Equilibrium between incentive to innovate and access to innovations. *Trade-off*: static efficiency vs. dynamic efficiency. Financial and fiscal incentives; promotion of technological entrepreneurship. *Technology-push* and *demand-pull* instruments of policy.

Introduction

Innovation policy deals with all actions of policymakers intended to influence the processes connected with the generation and diffusion of innovation. These processes go hand in hand with the complexity and uncertainty inherent to changing socio-economic systems. Innovation policy can be designed for the regional[27], the national or the supranational level, *e.g.* for EU level.

---

[27] By region we understand every entity that comprises a sub-national geographic unit smaller than a country. These units are normally closely interconnected with the national and global level and develop dynamically in this context. They can be characterized by internal coherence and can to some extent act as a collective entity, as stated in the regional innovation system approach.

Due to the globalization process and the liberalization of financial markets, budgetary and monetary policies are getting less autonomy. For this reason, labor market policy, social policy, infrastructure policy, education policy and, principally, innovation policy is becoming even more important. These are important factors for sustainable economic growth. If regions or firms do not have any innovation and learning, they will be unable to establish sustainable growth. Innovation represents a potential source of dynamic comparative advantages by enhancing the learning abilities of firms and workers. However, the private sector invests too little in R&D from society's perspective. Why?

Investments in R&D have very high returns and are a key component of economic growth. Under different assumptions, economic theory can explain why firms may under-invest or over-invest in R&D. Empirical research, however, demonstrates that the private sector invests less than the optimal level in R&D. Some authors estimate that total R&D spending in the economy is less than one quarter the optimal level. Under-investment occurs because firms cannot appropriate all the returns to their R&D investments and because capital market imperfections may make financing R&D more expensive than other investments.

From the firm's perspective, R&D is like any other investment. The firm invests in R&D until the expected risk-adjusted private returns of the last research project equals its costs. Average returns on R&D to the firm are high. Authors' estimations are around 20% to 30%, on average, but because of positive externalities returns to society are even higher: often 50% or more. These R&D spillovers occur as others use research results and extend them in directions the original innovator often could not have imagined. The existence of spillovers means that an innovator is compensated for only a fraction of the total returns on R&D. As a result, firms invest less in R&D than they would if they reaped all the rewards to their investments. In other words, some research projects that would yield positive net total benefits (*i.e.*, the sum of private return and spillover benefits less the project costs) are privately unprofitable because the investor does not see the value of spillovers. Without some intervention in the market, the private sector will not undertake these research projects, even though it is in the society's interest for them to do so.

In addition to investing in less R&D than the society would like, firms may invest less than they want if they do not have sufficient access to capital for R&D. Capital market failures could arise if an innovator is reluctant or unable to provide financiers with enough information to evaluate a research project for fear of revealing too much about the proposed idea. Moreover, R&D cannot be guaranteed, unlike investments in machines or buildings. Firms may therefore be forced to pay higher rates of interest on loans for R&D than charged borrowers financing other guaranteed forms of investment, or they may have to rely more extensively on internal funds.

Because funds are fungible, firms with sufficient internal cash flow can, of course, make use of those funds for research, using guarantees to finance investments in plant and equipment. The fact of the matter is that many high tech firms would like to invest more in research than they can finance through cash flow and guaranteed loans. Schumpeter called attention to these constraints long ago. The evidence of the impact of changes in cash flow on R&D investment, however, must be interpreted with caution, because events that adversely affect cash flow may also adversely affect the firm's net value and ability to accept risks. So, section 7.1 deals with foundations of the innovation policy, with special emphasis on the "appropriability problem", and presents a framework to compare the private with the social return of R&D projects.

When others reap the benefits of someone else's new ideas, market forces alone are unlikely to generate the optimal level of investment in knowledge — implying a need for government intervention. With such purpose, governments have provided for systems of IPR (intellectual property rights) in order to protect those who invest in knowledge from imitators and plagiarists. Temporary monopoly rights provide an incentive to invest in research by creating the potential to profit off an innovation before others can use it.

Patents, however, entail a high social cost. So, section 7.2 deals with the intellectual property problematic and the use of patents in innovation policy, while section 7.3 focuses on other innovation policy instruments.

7.1. Foundations of innovation policy

Why is a policy needed? The main motivation for an innovation policy is the chronic condition of under-investment in scientific and technological research by the private sector. This under-investment is due to market-failures that are associated to some deficiencies, such as the "appropriability problem". But there are other market-failures associated to uncertainty, risk aversion and information asymmetry, which produce imperfections in the capital market.

7.1.1. The "appropriability problem"

The potential value of an idea to any individual buyer generally would not match its value to the social multitude, since the latter would be the *sum* of the incremental benefits that members of the society derived from their individual use of the idea. Once a new bit of knowledge is revealed by its discoverer(s), some benefits will instantly spill over to others who are therefore able to share in its possession at little incremental cost. So, the discoverer of a new piece of knowledge has an "appropriability problem": he cannot appropriate all the benefits of its ingenuity.

The "appropriability problem" exists because we are dealing with public goods. Public goods have 2 important characteristics, which distinguish them from private goods: First, they are "non-rival in use", or have the property of "infinite expansibility", or the ability to generate "inter-temporal knowledge spillovers"; second, they are non-excludable, or they have a costly exclusion of others from possession. In the presence of public goods, the *competitive* market processes will not do an efficient (i.e. close to the social optimum) job of allocating resources for their production and distribution.

Although Romer (1990) has considered that knowledge has the public good characteristic of non-rivalry, in that the use of a piece of knowledge by one agent does not decrease the opportunity for other agents to use simultaneously the same piece, he highlights above all the need of excluding others from reaping the results of innovation, because if a firm invests in knowledge, spending money in R&D, it must recoup the return of such investment, in order to go on researching and so contributing to the enlargement of the basis of growth. So, a means of limiting the economic appropriation of the results of others' research is needed.

But the properties of non-rivalry and non-excludability also suggest that the market may fail to allocate sufficient resources to knowledge generation because individuals have difficulty in establishing and enforcing property rights over their new ideas – some of the benefits of an innovation are likely to accrue to others. So even if knowledge is not considered a pure public good it can produce positive externalities causing that the private return to innovation is less than the social return. Facing such market failure, economics teaches us that governments need to subsidize R&D.

Contracting for the creation of information goods (the specifications of which may be stipulated but do not yet exist) is troubled with still greater risks; and, *a fortiori*, fundamental uncertainties surround transactional arrangements involving efforts to produce truly novel discoveries and inventions. In fact information asymmetries make the effects of the "appropriability problem" more severe. But the uncertainty that surrounds the R&D projects originates another market-failure. Firstly, the value of basic research is more conjectural than that of applied research, and is therefore more likely to be undervalued by private firms and individuals. Private firms and individuals are likely to be more risk adverse than they would be if acting collectively through the government, and so they may avoid undertaking basic research to any large extent because of its greater uncertainty. Secondly, imperfections in the capital market that leave researchers asset-constrained, particularly when facing the likelihood that an exploratory project will have an extended duration and a long wait before results can be exploited commercially, is a source of "R&D market failure" per se, moreover when the researcher, the innovator and the financier are distinct entities.

7.1.2. Social rate vs. private rate of return of innovative activities

Figure 7.1, on the next page, can help us illustrate the problem of differences between private return and social evaluation. Each point (A, B, C, D, E) represents the investment needed to implement an innovative project. The 45 degrees line represents the equality between private and social rates of return. So, projects positioned above the line have positive externalities while projects below the line have negative externalities.

In innovative actions, it is usually considered that social benefits can exceed private benefits and that there will be no negative externalities. So, innovative or knowledge based investments will appear always above the 45 degrees line. For instance, A can illustrate a project with a private return equal to the social return, i.e., a project without externalities. But, this is a project that should not be implemented because its expected return is below the minimum required, both by the private sector (it is below the private hurdle rate) and by the government (it is lower than the social hurdle rate).

Figure 7.1.
Private and social return rates of innovative projects

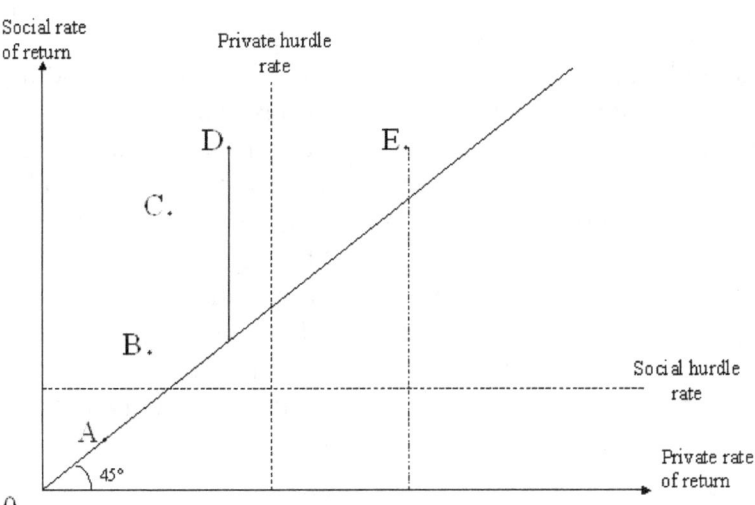

On the other hand, project D illustrates a basic R&D project for which private return is very low (under the private hurdle rate) and, at the same time, social return is very high, i.e., the social benefits will spread all over the country or even outside, as it is often the case. So, this project, which is not profitable in a private point of view and so there is no private firm that take it in hand, should be supported by public policy because of its high social value. Project E illustrates an investment, which is profitable from the private point of view, and so can be implemented by the private sector. However, this investment produces lower externalities (spillovers) than the project D.

7.2. The intellectual property problematic and the use of patents

Intellectual property rights such as patents, copyrights, and registered trademarks are the base for building and extending the markets for new technologies, i.e. innovations. The specification and enforcement of private rights to market a firm's product is vital in almost all industries, partly because it is becoming easier and cheaper to copy new technologies. Intellectual property rights are in the long run promoting economic growth, technology transfer and local innovation. Intellectual property rights have the characteristics of being negative, *i.e.* they are rights that limit other parties in their behavior, they stop pirates, imitations, counterfeiters, and in some cases limit third parties that have independently reached the same ideas from using them without a license from the right-owner.

Patents provide the inventor with a monopoly on his invention for a given time period. In theory, and often also in practice, patents solve the problem of fully appropriating the returns when R&D is successful and generates an invention. Patents obstruct a wider use of the invention and restrict the diffusion of technological knowledge. Thus, patents may be an impediment, especially when the returns from knowledge diffusion are high. Some authors even reject the patenting of academic research in order to stimulate commercial applications, and argue instead that public expenditures for fundamental scientific research should be increased.

7.2.1. Equilibrium between incentive to innovate and access to innovations

Why does the law protect inventions and artistic works? The answer is that intellectual property law seeks to encourage innovation and creation, while enabling access. This basic principle is highlighted by the economic analysis, which assimilates works of the intellect to the production of information, although this presents two problems in terms of allocation of resources[28].

Firstly, information is a non-excludable good. This means that it is impossible to exclude an individual from using the good even if he does not contribute to the cost of producing it. For example, a publisher cannot stop the same book from being loaned and read by several people. Similarly, a newspaper journalist cannot prevent an original piece of information from being repeated by colleagues. The practical problem posed by these goods is the lack of incentive for entrepreneurs to produce them. From the outset, they know they will have difficulty being paid and covering their costs. From the point of view of the community, there is a loss in welfare because goods for which there is a potential user will not be produced.

Secondly, information is a non-rival good. When an individual consumes information, this act does not reduce the quantity available to other people. For example, watching a football game on television does not prevent other viewers from consuming the same program. Non-rivalry can be seen as the opposite of congestion. The enjoyment of watching a football game is not diminished by the presence of a large number of other viewers around the world. In other words, the marginal cost of serving an additional consumer is zero. Consequently, when a producer charges for his service, consumption of the good is needlessly reduced. Consumers whose willingness to pay is lower than the available price are excluded from using the good, although they would have benefited from it at no cost to anyone. Social welfare is not maximized.

By offering an exclusive right for a limited period, intellectual property law addresses these two problems sequentially. Initially, the legal mechanism of protection makes the good excludable. Users are required to pay for the services offered through fees. Subsequently,

---

[28] See Arrow (1962).

when the work passes into the public domain, all consumers can access it free of charge.

7.2.2. *Trade-off*: static efficiency vs. dynamic efficiency

By addressing the problems of non-excludability and non-rivalry of information sequentially, patents and copyright are necessarily imperfect mechanisms. During the period of protection, the rationing of consumption generates a deadweight loss for society. Once a work passes into public domain, the deadweight loss disappears, but the innovators lose their royalties, which may prevent innovations that would benefit society from being produced. Let us consider, for example, an invention with a cost of 100, a value to society of 150, from which the company can derive annual revenue of 4 per year. The invention is socially useful because its value is higher than its cost.

If the property right lasts for 20 years, it is not profitable for the company to make the corresponding investment in R&D. At the end of the 20 years period the company is able to recoup only 80 of the 100 initially spent. In other words, to limit the problem of non-excludability, the period of legal protection must be infinite, whereas to eliminate the problem of non-rivalry it must be zero. However, the government must assure the general interest and thus intellectual property law must attempt to strike a balance between the incentive to create and innovate, and the benefits of diffuse the results obtained. This contradiction between incentive and use translates into economic language as a *trade-off* between dynamic and static efficiency.

To sum up, knowledge is a public good in the sense that the marginal cost of an additional individual using that knowledge is zero. There is thus a trade-off between static inefficiency, associated with the underutilization of knowledge, and dynamic inefficiency, associated with the underproduction of knowledge. That is, once knowledge has been produced, it is inefficient to prevent others from using it, but if anyone can use it without cost, there will be little incentive to undertake the investments necessary to produce that knowledge. The rules for intellectual property rights attempt to strike a balance, for example, by choosing the length of the patent's life and the breadth of the discovery the patent covers.

7.3. Other policy instruments

7.3.1. *Technology-push* instruments, or *demand-pull* instruments?

A possible taxonomy for innovation policy separates government actions that affect the size of the market for a new technology from those that influence the supply of new knowledge. Governments can thus encourage innovation in two ways: they can implement measures that reduce the private cost of producing innovation, i.e. *technology-push* instruments, and they can implement measures that increase the private payoff to successful innovation, i.e. *demand-pull* instruments.

Examples of public policies that reduce the cost to firms of producing innovation include: government sponsored R&D, tax credits for companies to invest in R&D enhancing the capacity for knowledge exchange, support for education and training, and funding demonstration projects. Knowledge spillover externalities provide the most prominent justification for such actions (Jones and Williams, 1998). Critics of policies that use *technology-push* instruments note their mixed record of success, the possibility that public spending crowds-out private investment, and their tendency to isolate scientific understanding from technical knowledge.

Examples of government actions that raise the payoffs for successful innovations include: intellectual property protection, tax credits and discounts for consumers of new technologies, government procurement, technology mandates, regulatory standards, and taxes on competing technologies. It is obvious that the type of innovation conditions the adoption and effectiveness of policy instruments. There is some empirical evidence suggesting that incremental innovation is more likely to respond to demand-pull than technology-push, and that non-incremental innovation is more responsive to technology-push (Dosi, 1988).

7.3.2. The need to consider the type of R&D and the type of knowledge

Part of the conventional market failure justification offered for government intervention in the sphere of scientific and technological R&D recognizes a difference between "fundamental" or "basic" research on the one hand, and "applied" or "commercially oriented" R&D, on the other. The special need to subsidize the former has been found in its greater level of uncertainty, and the longer time horizons over which research programs of that kind generally need to be sustained. This line of argument, however, does not adequately account for the existence of two quite different organizational and incentive mechanisms that government policies maintain in order to provide economic support for research activities. More recent institutional analysis associated with the so-called "new economics of science" has offered a functionalist explanation for the "open" part of the institutional complex of modern science, which traditionally was (and in many countries still is) closely associated with the carry out of research in public institutes and universities.

The difficulty of monitoring research effort forces both the open science system and the intellectual property regime to tie researchers' rewards in one way or another to priority in the production of observable "research outputs" that can be submitted to "validity testing and valorization" – whether directly by peer assessment (in basic science), or indirectly through their application in the markets for goods and services (in "commercially oriented" R&D).

The modern rationale for public policies supporting "open science" focuses on the economic and social efficiency aspects of rapid and complete information disclosure for the pursuit of knowledge, and the supportive role played by informal and institutionalized norms that tend to reinforce cooperative behavior among scientists. It highlights the "incentive compatibility" of the key norm of disclosure within a collegiate reputation-based reward system that is grounded upon validated claims to priority in discovery or invention. In brief, rapid disclosure facilitates the rapid validation of findings, reduces excessive duplication of research effort, enlarges the domain of complementarities and creates beneficial "spillovers" among research programs.

The two distinctive organizational regimes thus serve quite different purposes that are complementary and highly rewarding when they co-exist at the macro-institutional level. This functional combination suggests a logical explanation for their co-existence, and the maintenance of institutional and cultural separations between the communities of researchers forming the 'Republic of Science' and those engaged in commercially oriented R&D conducted under proprietary rules.

7.3.3. Policy instruments to support R&D: financial and fiscal incentives; promotion of technological entrepreneurship.

As previously stated, the existence of market failures opens up the possibility for governments to help mitigate the under-investment problem. Governments have traditionally used many tools to promote science and technology. Some methods, such as the patent system and research tax credits, are indirect. The patent system is probably the oldest tool for promoting R&D, as it increases the potential profits from an innovation. The patent system grants a temporary monopoly to an innovator because an innovation is costly to develop but often inexpensive to duplicate.

Research tax credits, a much newer mechanism, decrease the cost of doing research to the firm by giving the firm a tax credit for a portion of its R&D expenditures. A credit provides an incentive to increase R&D investment by reducing the cost of any research project, making any given project potentially more profitable. The R&D tax credit is actually a credit on incremental expenditures. As such, its impact on the long-run level of expenditures might be expected to be more limited. There are also concerns about whether all expenditures qualifying for the incremental R&D tax credit really are research and development (e.g., should marketing research really qualify for the tax credit?). The R&D credit, of course, does not attempt to distinguish between research that has a high level of spillovers and research that does not.

Governments also directly fund R&D. As noted above, the governments fund the majority of basic research, where market failures are presumably greatest. Much of governmental support for basic research goes to universities and public institutes. Basic research is crucial for long-run growth, and is a key ingredient in more applied R&D. Commercial products and innovations, however, are rarely the stimulus for basic research and often come years after the research is completed. For that reason, and because commercial applications of basic research are rarely obvious, firms have little incentive to fund basic research on their own.

So, there is little disagreement that governments must take the lead in funding basic research and training scientists (presumably because the total returns to society from their activities are in excess of the returns they appropriate). Much of government-direct R&D funding goes to applied R&D in industry, although the extent to which government should support industrial R&D is more controversial. Traditionally, most of this funding has been to satisfy government objectives like defense, and, especially in recent times, health research directly. Although market failures may be less extreme in applied R&D than in basic research, they still exist. Even the most applied R&D is inherently risky and can generate large spillovers.

Governmental support of R&D has generally been successful in helping to mitigate the under-investment problem. Each dollar in research tax credit appears to generate more than a dollar in private R&D spending. Direct government spending also seems to stimulate additional private spending on both basic and applied research. Although most public R&D was not intended to yield commercial products for civilian use, it would often spin off into commercial use.

*

*   *

Exercises and review questions

7.1 The existence of market failures opens up the possibility that government can help diminish the under-investment problem. Why does market fail in allocating sufficient resources to innovation?

7.2. Intellectual property law must attempt to strike a balance between the incentive to create and innovate, and the benefits of diffusing the results obtained. In other words, policy faces a *trade-off* between dynamic and static efficiency. Explain why this trade-off exists.

7.3. Go to page 151 and look at figure 7.1. Why is the private hurdle rate of return represented as higher than the private hurdle rate of return in the figure?

*

*   *

BIBLIOGRAPHY

Abramovitz, Moses (1986), "Catching-up, Forging Ahead and falling Behind", *Journal of Economic History*, volume 46, n° 2, pp. 385-406.

Arrow KJ (1962) The economic implications of learning by doing. *Review of Economic Studies* 29: 155–173.

Asheim, Bjørn and Gertler, Meric (2005), "The Geography of Innovation", in Jan Fagerberg, David C. Mowery, and Richard R. Nelson (eds) (2006), *The Oxford Handbook of Innovation*, Ch. 11, 291-317.

Baptista, Rui and Peter Swann (1998). Do firms in clusters innovate more?, *Research Policy* 27, pp. 525–540.

Baumol, William J. (2002), *The Free-Market Innovation Machine: Analysing the Growth Miracle of Capitalism*, Princeton, New Jersey: Princeton University Press.

Beaudry C, Schiffauerova A (2009), Who's right, Marshall or Jacobs? The localization versus urbanization debate. *Research Policy* 38: 318–337.

Beccatinni, G. (1992), Le District Marshallien: une Notion Socio-économique in Benko, G. and A. Lipietz (eds) Les Régions qui Gagnent: Districts et Réseaux. Les Nouveaux Paradigmes de la Géographie Économique. Paris : PUF.

Bell, M. and Pavitt, K. (1997), "Technological Accumulation and industrial growth: contrasts between developed and developing countries", in Archibugi and Michie (1997), *Technology, Globalisation and Economic Performance*, Cambridge University Press.

Boschma, R. (2005). "Proximity and Innovation: A Critical Assessment", *Regional Studies* 39(1) pp. 61-74.

Brachert, Matthias, Mirko Titze and Alexander Kubis (2011), Identifying industrial clusters from a multidimensional perspective: Methodical aspects with an application to Germany, *Papers in Regional Science*, Volume 90 Number 2, pp. 419-40.

Braun, E., MacDonald, S. (1978) *Revolution in Miniature: The history and impact of semiconductor electronics*. Cambridge: Cambridge University Press.

Buerger, Matthias and Uwe Cantner (2011). The regional dimension of sectoral innovativeness: An empirical investigation of two specialized suppliers and two science-based industries, *Papers in Regional Science*, Volume 90 Number 2 June 2011, pp. 373-394.

Camagni, Roberto (1991),"Local Milieu, uncertainty and innovation networks: towards a new dynamic theory of economic space", in R. Camagni (1991) (ed.), *Innovation Networks: spatial perspectives*, London: Belhaven Press.

Ciccone, A. 2002. Agglomeration Effects in Europe, *European Economic Review*, 46: 213-227.

Ciccone, A. and R. E. Hall, 1996. Productivity and the Density of Economic Activity. *American Economic Review*, 86 (1): 54-70.

Coe, David, and Elhanan Helpman (1995), "International R&D Spillovers." *European Economic Review, Vol.* 39(5), pp. 859-87.

Coe, David, Elhanan Helpman and Alexander Hoffmaister (1997), "North-South R&D Spillovers", *Economic Journal*, Vol. 107, pp. 134-49.

Cooke P (2001) Clusters as key determinants of economic growth: The example of biotechnology. In: Mariussen A (ed) *Cluster policies – cluster development?* Nordregio Report 2001/2, Stockholm.

David, P. A. and J. L. Rosenbloom (1990), Marshallian factor market externalities and the dynamics of industrial location. *Journal of Urban Economics* 28, pp. 349–370.

de Groot, H. L. F., Poot, J. & Smit, M. J. (2008). Agglomeration externalities, innovation and regional growth: Theoretical perspectives and meta-analysis. (Department of Economics Working Paper Series, Number 1/08). Hamilton, New Zealand: University of Waikato.

162

De Long, Bradford and Summers, Lawrence (1993), "How Strongly Do Developing Economies Benefit from Equipment Investment?", *Journal of Monetary Economics*, vol. 23, pp. 395-415.

Dosi, Giovanni (1982), "Technical paradigms and technological trajectories: A suggested interpretation of the determinants of technical change". *Research Polic*y, Vol. II(3), pp. 147-162.

Dosi, Giovanni (1984), *Technical Change and Industrial Transformation*, London: Macmillan.

Dosi Giovanni (1988), "Sources, procedures and microeconomic effects of innovation", *Journal of Economic Literatur*e, Vol. 26, pp. 1120-117.

Dosi, Giovanni (1997), "Opportunities, Incentives and the Collective Patterns of Technological Change", *The Economic Journal*, Vol. 107, pp. 1530-47.

Dosi, G., C. Freeman, R. Nelson, Silverberg and L. Soete (eds.) (1988), *Technical Change and Economic Theor*y, London: Pinter; New York: Columbia University Press.

Duranton, Gilles and Diego Puga (2001). "Nursery Cities: Urban Diversity, Process Innovation, and the Life Cycle of Products," *American Economic Review*, vol. 91(5), pages 1454-1477.

Edquist C. (1997) "Systems of innovation approaches - their emergence and characteristics" in Edquist, C. (ed.) (1997) *Systems of Innovation: Technologies, Institutions and Organizations,* London: Pinter/Cassell.

Edquist, C. and Johnson, B. (1997), 'Institutions and organisations in systems of innovation', in C. Edquist (ed.) *Systems of Innovation: Technologies, Institutions and Organizations.* London and Washington: Pinter/Cassell Academic.

Enright M. (1996) Regional clusters and economic development: A research agenda. In: Staber U, Schaefer N V, Sharma B (eds) *Business networks: Prospects for regional development.* De Gruyter, New York.

Fagerberg, Jan (1987), "A Technology Gap Approach to Why Growth Rates Differ", *Research Policy*, Vol. 16(2-4), pp. 87-99, reedited in C. Freeman (1990), *The Economics of Innovation*, Edward Elgar.

Fagerberg, Jan (1988), "Why Growth Rates Differ". In Giovanni Dosi, *et al.* (eds.), *Technical Change and Economic Theory*, London: Pinter, pp. 432-57.

Fagerberg, Jan and Bart Verspagen (2002) Technology-gaps, innovation-diffusion and transformation: an evolutionary interpretation, *Research Policy*, Volume 31 (8-9), pp. 1291-1304.

Feldman, M. (2000) Location and Innovation: the new economic Geography of innovation, spillovers, and agglomeration. In GL Clark, M. Feldman, and M. Gertler (eds.). *Oxford Handbook of Economic Geography*. Oxford: Oxford University Press, pp. 373-394.

Feldman, M, and Audretsch D. B. (1999), Innovation in cities: science-based diversity, specialization and localized competition. *European Economic Review* 43(2): 409–429.

Florida, R. (2002), Bohemia and Economic Geography, *Journal of Economic Geography* 2: 55-71.

Florida, R. (2002a), Bohemia and Economic Geography, *Journal of Economic Geography* 2. pp. 55-71.

Florida, R. (2002b), *The Rise of the Creative Class – and how it's transforming work, leisure, community, & everyday life*. The Perseus Books Group, New York.

Florida, R. (2002c), The Economic Geography of Talent. *Annals of the Association of American Geographers,* 92:743-755.

Florida, R. (2004), America's Looming Creativity Crisis. *Harvard Business Review* 82:122-136.

Florida, R. (2005a), *The Flight of the Creative Class*. Harper Business, New York.

Florida, R (2005b) *Cities and the Creative Class*. Routledge, New York and London.

Florida, R. and Gates, G. (2002) Technology and Tolerance – Diversity and High-Tech Growth, *The Brooking Review*, Winter, 20:32-36.

Freeman, C. (1982). *The Economics of Industrial Innovation*. London, Pinter Publishers.

Freeman, C. (1987). *Technology policy and economic performance: lessons from Japan*. London: Pinter.

Freeman, C. (2004), "Technological infrastructure and international competitiveness", Industrial and Corporate Change, volume 13(3), pp. 541-569.

Freeman, C. and L. Soete (1990), "Fast Structural Change and Slow Productivity Change: Some Paradoxes in the Economics of Information Technology." *Structural Change and Economic Dynamics* 1: 225-242.

Freeman, C. and L. Soete (1997), *The Economics of Industrial Innovation*. 3rd Edition. London and Washington, Pinter.

Freeman, C., J. Clark, and L. Soete. (1982), *Unemployment and Technical Innovation*, London, Pinter.

Frenken, K., FG Van Oort, and T. Verburg (2007). Related variety, unrelated variety and regional economic growth, *Regional Studies* 41(5): 685-697.

Fujita M., P. Krugman and A. J. Venables (1999), *The Spatial Economy: Cities, Regions, and International Trade*, MIT press.

Gertler M (2003), Tacit knowledge and the economic geography of context, or the undefinable tacitness of being (there). *Journal of economic geography* 3(1): 75-99.

Glaeser Edward L, and David Maré (2001), Cities and Skills, *Journal of Labor Economics*. April; Vol. 19(2):316–342.

Glaeser, E. L. and J. D. Gottlieb (2009), The Wealth of Cities: Agglomeration Economies and Spatial Equilibrium in the United States. *Journal of Economic Literature*, 47: 983-1028.

Glaeser, Edward L., Hedi D. Kallal, Jose A. Scheinkman andAndrei Shleifer, 1992. "Growth in Cities," *Journal of Political Economy*, vol. 100(6), pages 1126-52

Grabher, G. (1993) The weakness of strong ties: the 'lock-in' of regional development in the Ruhr area. In G. Grabher (ed.) *The Embedded*

Firm: On the Socio-economics of Industrial Networks, pp. 255–277. London: Routledge.

Griliches, Zvi (1990), "Patent Statistics as Economic Indicators: A Survey", *Journal of Economic Literature,* Vol. 28, pp. 1661-1707.

Griliches, Zvi (1992), "The Search for R&D Spillovers", *Scandinavian Journal of Economics,* Vol. 94, Suplement, pp 29-47.

Griliches, Zvi (1994), "Productivity, R&D, and the Data Constraint", *The American Economic Review*, Vol. 84(1), pp. 1-23.

Grossman, Gene and Elhanan Helpman (1991), *Innovation and Growth in the Global Economy.* Cambridge, Mass.: MIT Press.

Hall, Bronwyn H. and Beethika Khan (2003), Adoption of New Technology. NBER Working Paper 9730 (available at http://www.nber.org/papers/w9730).

Hall, Peter (1993), *Innovation, Economics and Evolution: Theoretical Perspectives on Changing Technology in Economic Systems*, New York: Harvester Wheatsheaf.

Henderson, V., A. Kuncoro and M. Turner (1995), Industrial development in cities. *Journal of Political Economy* 103, pp. 1067–1085.

Henning, M., J. Moodysson & M. Nilsson (2010), *Innovation and regional transformation: from clusters to new combinations.* Malmö: Region Skåne.

Hounshell, D.A. (1984), *From the American System to Mass Production, 1800-1932.* Baltimore: The Johns Hopkins University Press.

Huang, Z., X. Zhang, and Y. Zhu. 2008. The role of clustering in rural industrialization: A case study of Wenzhou's footwear industry. *China Economic Review* 19: 409–420.

IIT, 1968. *Technology in retrospect and critical events in science (project TRACES).* Report, Illinois Institute of Technology (IIT) – National Science Foundation.

Isaksen A (1997), Regional clusters and competitiveness: The Norwegian case. *European Planning Studies* 5: 65–76.

Jacobs, J. (1961) *The Death and Life of Great American Cities*, New York: Random House.

Jacobs, J. (1969), *The Economy of Cities*, Penguin, London.

Jacobs, J. (1984), *Cities and the Wealth of Nations: Principles of Economic Life*, Vintage, New York.

Jaffe, A., Trajtenberg, M., Henderson, R. (1993), Geographic localization of knowledge spillovers as evidenced by patent citations. *Quarterly Journal of Economics* 108 (3), 577–598.

Jones, Charles I. and J. C. Williams (1998), Measuring The Social Return To R&D, *The Quarterly Journal of Economics,* 113, 1119-1135.

Keeble, D., Wilkinson, F. (Eds.) (2000) *High-Technology Clusters, Networking and Collective Learning in Europe*. Ashgate, Aldershot.

Kennedy, Charles (1964), "Induced Bias in Innovation and the Theory of Distribution", *The Economic Journal*, Vol. 74, pp. 541-7.

Kennedy, Charles (1966), "Samuelson on Induced Innovation", *Review of Economics and Statistics*, Vol. 48, pp. 442-4.

Ketelhöhn, Niels W. (2006), The role of clusters as sources of dynamic externalities in the US semiconductor industry, *Journal of Economic Geography*, 6 (5): 679-699.

Kline, S.J. and N. Rosenberg (1986), "An overview of innovation." In R. Landau and N. Rosenberg (eds.), *The Positive Sum Strategy: Harnessing Technology for Economic Growth*. Washington, D.C.: National Academy Press, pp. 275–305.

Kondratieff, N. D. (1935), The Long Waves In Economic Life, The *Review of Economic Statistics*, volume XVII (6), 105-115.

Krugman, P. (1991), *Geography and trade*. Cambridge, MA: MIT Press.

Leslie, S. W. (2000), The biggest "Angel" of them all: the military and the making of Silicon Valley. In M. Kenney (ed.) *Understanding Silicon Valley: The Anatomy of an Entrepreneurial Region*. Stanford, CA: Stanford University Press, 48–67.

Lévêque, François and Yann Ménière (2004), *The Economics of Patents and Copyright*, Berkeley Electronic Press.

Lundvall, B-Å. (ed.) (1992), *National Systems of Innovation: Towards a Theory of Innovation and Interactive learning*, London: Pinter.

167

Lundvall, Bengt-Ake *et al.* (2002), "National systems of production, innovation and competence building", *Research Policy*, volume 31, pp. 213-231.

Macher, J. T., Mowery, D. C., Hodges, D. A. (1998), Reversal of fortune? The recovery of the US semiconductor industry. *California Management Review*, 41: 107–136.

Malerba, Franco and Luigi Orsenigo (1995). "Schumpeterian Patterns of Innovation," *Cambridge Journal of Economics*, vol. 19(1), pages 47-65.

Malmberg, Anders and Maskell, Peter (2002), The elusive concept of localization economies: towards a knowledge-based theory of spatial clustering. *Environment and Planning A* 34 (3), 429–449.

Malmberg, Anders and Maskell, Peter (2006), "Localized Learning Revisited." *Growth and Change* 37(1): 1-18.

Marshall, A. (1920), *Principles of Economics* (8th ed.) London: Macmillan. (Original work published 1890)

Martin, R. and Sunley, P. (2003). "Deconstructing Clusters: Chaotic Concept or Policy Panacea?" *Journal of Economic Geography*, 3 (1), pp. 5-35.

Maskell P. and A Malmberg (1999), Localised learning and industrial competitiveness, *Cambridge Journal of Economics*, 23 (2), 167-185.

Maskell, P., Eskelinen, H., Hannibalsson, I., Malmberg, A. and Vatne, E. (1998), *Competitiveness, localised learning and regional development. Specialisation and prosperity in small open economies*, London: Routledge

Morgan, Kevin (2004), "The exaggerated death of geography: learning, proximity and territorial innovation systems" *Journal of Economic Geography*, 4, pp. 3-21.

Morris, P. R. (1990), *A History of the World's Semiconductor Industry*. London: Peter Peregrinus Ltd.

Mowery, D. C. and Nathan Rosenberg (1989), "The Influence of Market Demand upon Innovation: a Critical Review of some Recent Empirical Studies", *Research Policy*, Vol. 8, pp. 102-53.

Neffke F, Henning M, Boschma R, Lundquist K-J, Olander L-O (2011), The dynamics of agglomeration externalities along the life cycle of industries. *Regional Studies* 45: 49–65.

Neffke, Frank, Martin Svensson Henning, and Ron Boschma (2008), "Surviving in agglomerations: Plant evolution and the changing benefits of the local environment," Papers in Evolutionary Economic Geography (PEEG) 0820, Utrecht University, Section of Economic Geography.

Nelson, Richard R. (ed.) (1962), *The Rate and Direction of Inventive Activity*, Princeton: Princeton University Press, NBER.

Nelson, R. R. (1988), The Agenda for growth theory: a different point of view, *Cambridge Journal of Economics*, 497-520.

Nelson, R. R. (1993) (ed.). *National Innovation Systems: A Comparative Study*, Oxford: Oxford University Press.

Nelson, R. R. (1995), "Recent evolutionary theorizing about economic change", *Journal of Economic Literature*, volume 33, pp.48-90.

Nelson, R.R. (2004), "The Market Economy and the scientific commons", *Research Policy*, volume 33, pp.455-471.

Nelson, R.R. and Pack, Howard (1998), "The Asian Miracle and Modern Growth Theory", Policy Research Working Paper n° 1881, Washington: World Bank.

Nelson, R. and E. Phelps (1966), "Investment in Humans, Technological Diffusion, and Economic Growth", *American Economic Review*, Vol. 61, pp. 69-75.

Nelson, R.R. and Winter, S. (1982), *An Evolutionary Theory of Economic Change*, Cambridge, M.A.: Harvard University Press.

Nilsson, Magnus (2008). A Tale of Two Clusters: Sharing Resources to Compete. Department of Business Administration. Lund, Lund University. PhD: 349.

Nordhaus, William D. (1973), "Some Skeptical Thoughts on the Theory of Induced Innovation", *Quarterly Journal of Economics*, Vol. 87, pp. 208-19.

OECD (1990), "Proposed Standard Method of Compiling and Interpreting Technology Balance of Payments Data: TBP Manual 1990", The Measurement of Scientific and Technological Activities Series, Paris.

OECD (1992), *Technology and the Economy: The Key Relationships*, Paris: OECD.

OECD (1994), "Using Patent Data as Science and Technology Indicators – Patent Manual: The Measurement of Scientific and Technological Activities", OCDE/ GD(94)114,1994, Paris.

OECD (1996), *The Measurement of Scientific and Technical Activities: Proposed Guidelines for Collecting and Interpreting Technological Innovation Data: Oslo Manual* (DSTI, OECD, Paris).

OECD (2002). *Proposed Standard Practice for Surveys of Research and Experimental Development: Frascati Manual. The Measurement of Scientific and Technical Activities Series.* Paris: Organisation for Economic Co-operation and Development.

Okubo, Y. (1997), "Bibliometric Indicators and Analysis of Research Systems, Methods and Examples", OECD, STI Working Paper 1997/1, Paris.

Pack. Howard (2000), "Industrial policy: growth elixir or poison", The World Bank Research Observer, volume 15, n°1, pp. 47-67.

Pavitt, K. (1984), "Sectoral Patterns of Technical Change: Towards a Taxonomy and a Theory", *Research Policy*, volume 13, pp. 343-373

Perez, C. (1983). "Structural change and the assimilation of new technologies in the economic and social systems." *Futures* **15**: 357-75.

Perez, C. (1985), "Microelectronics, long waves and world structural change: New perspectives for developing countries", *World Development*, Vol. 13(3), pp. 441-63.

Perry, Martin (2010a), *Controversies in Local Economic Development: Stories, Strategies, Solutions.* Abingdon: Routledge.

Perry, Martin (2010b), "Controversies in Local Economic Development". *Local Economy*, 25(7): 527-534.

Pessoa, Argentino (2005), "Ideas" driven growth: the OECD evidence. *Portuguese Economic Journal* **4**, 46-67.

Pessoa, Argentino (2010), "R&D and economic growth: How strong is the link?" *Economics Letters*, vol. **107(2)**, pp. 152-154.

Piore, M. J., and C. F. Sabel (1984), *The second industrial divide: Possibilities for prosperity*. New York: Basic Books.

Polanyi, M. (1967), *The Tacit Dimension*. London, Routledge.

Porter, M. (1990), *The Competitive Advantage of Nations*. New York, United States: Free Press.

Porter, M. (1998), "Clusters versus Industrial Policy." In: M. Porter, editor. *On Competition*. Cambridge, United States: Harvard Business School Press.

Porter, M. (2000), Location, competition and economic development: local clusters in the global economy, *Economic Development Quarterly* **14**, 15-31.

Potter, Antony and H. Doug Watts (2011), Evolutionary agglomeration theory: increasing returns, diminishing returns, and the industry life cycle, *Journal of Economic Geography,* 11(3): 417-455.

Putnam, R.D. (1993), *Making Democracy Work: Civic Traditions in Modern Italy*. Princeton: Princeton Press.

Rodríguez-Clare, Andrés (2007), Clusters and comparative advantage: Implications for industrial policy, *Journal of Development Economics*, Volume 82, Issue 1, Pages 43-57.

Romer, Paul M. (1986), Increasing returns and long-run growth. *The Journal of Political Economy* 94: 1002–1037.

Romer, Paul M. (1990), "Endogenous Technological Change", *Journal of Political Economy*, Vol. 98(5), pp. S71-102.

Rosenberg, N. (1976), *Perspectives on Technology*, Cambridge: Cambridge University Press.

Rosenberg, N. (1982), *Inside the Black Box: Technology and Economics*, Cambridge: Cambridge University Press.

Rosenberg, N. (1994), *Exploring the Black Box: Technology, Economics, and History*, Cambridge: Cambridge University Press.

Rosenberg, Nathan and C. Frischtak (1984), "Technological Innovation and long waves", *Cambridge Journal of Economics* 8 (1): 7-24.

Rosenfeld, Stuart (2005), Industry Clusters: Business Choice, Policy Outcome, or Branding Strategy? *Journal of New Business Ideas and Trends*, 3(2), pp. 4-13.

Rosenthal, S.S., and W.C. Strange (2004), "Evidence on the Nature and Sources of Agglomeration Economies." in J.V. Henderson, J.F. Thisse (eds) *Handbook of Urban and Regional Economics*. Volume 4. Amsterdam, The Netherlands: Elsevier Science Publishers, pp. 2119-2171.

Ruttan, Vernon W. (1997), "Induced Innovation, Evolutionary Theory and Path Dependence: Sources of Technical Change", *The Economic Journal, Vol.* 107, pp. 1520-9.

Saxenian, A. (1994), *Regional Advantage: Culture and Competition in Silicon Valley and Route 128*. Cambridge, MA: Harvard University Press.

Scherer, F.M. (1982), "Demand-Pull and Technological Innovation: Schmookler Revisited," *Journal of Industrial Economics* 30(3): 225-238.

Schmitz, H. (1995) Collective efficiency: Growth path for small-scale industry. *Journal of Development Studies* 31 (4): 529–566.

Schmookler, Jacob (1954), "The Level of Inventive Activity", *Review of Economics and Statistics*, Vol. 36(2), pp. 183-90.

Schmookler, Jacob (1957), "Inventors, Past and Present", *Review of Economics and Statistics*, Vol. 39(3), pp. 183-90.

Schmookler, Jacob (1962), "Determinants of Industrial Invention", in Richard R. Nelson (ed.), *The Rate and Direction of Inventive Activity: Economic and Social Factors*, Princeton: Princeton University Press.

Schmookler, Jacob (1966), *Invention and Economic Growth*, Cambridge, MA: Harvard University Press.

Schumpeter, J.A. (1911, 1934, 1936), *The theory of economic development*, Harvard University Press, Cambridge.

Schumpeter, J.A. (1928), The instability of capitalism, *Economic Journal* 38, 361-86.

Schumpeter, J.A. (1939), *Business cycles*, McGraw-Hill, New York.

Schumpeter, J.A. (1942), *Capitalism, socialism and democracy*, Harper and Brothers, New York.

Sherwin, C.W. and Isenson, R.S. (1967), Project HINDSIGHT. *Science* 156 (3782), 1571-1577.

Smith, T. W. (2000), Semiconductors. Standard & Poor's Industry Surveys, New York.

Solow, Robert M. (1957), "Technical change and the aggregate production function", *Review of Economics and Statistics*, Vol. 39(3), pp. 312-320.

Spencer G, Vinodrai T, Gertler M, and Wolfe D (2009), Do clusters make a difference? Defining and assessing their economic performance. *Regional Studies* 34: 1-19.

Steiner, M. (Ed.) (1998), *Clusters and Regional Specialisation: On Geography, Technology, and Networks*. London: Pion.

Stiglitz, Joseph E. (1987), "Learning to Learn, Localised Learning and Technological Progress", in Dasgupta and Stoneman (eds.), *Economic Policy and Technological Performance*, Cambridge University Press.

Storper, M. (1997), The Regional World. New York: The Guilford Press.

Storper, M. (2009), The economics of context, location and trade: another great transformation?. In G. Becattini, M. Bellandi, L. De Propris (eds) *The Handbook of Industrial Districts*, pp 141–157. Cheltenham: Edward Elgar.

Tödtling, Franz, Patrick Lehner, and Alexander Kaufmann (2009), Do different types of innovation rely on specific kinds of knowledge interactions? Technovation 29, 59–71.

UNU-MERIT (2012) *Innovation Union Scoreboard 2011: The Innovation Union's performance scoreboard for Research and Innovation* (available at http://www.proinno-europe.eu/metrics).

von Hippel, E. (1988), *The Sources of Innovation*, Oxford University Press.

von Hippel, E. (1994), "'Sticky Information' and the Locus of Problem Solving: Implications for Innovation", *Management Science* Vol. 40, pp. 429-439.

www.ingramcontent.com/pod-product-compliance
Lightning Source LLC
Chambersburg PA
CBHW081444170526
45166CB00008B/2306